Improving Productivity in State and Local Government

*A Statement
on National Policy
by the Research and Policy Committee
of the Committee
for Economic Development*

March 1976

Library of Congress Cataloging in Publication Data

Committee for Economic Development.
  Improving productivity in state and local government.

  Includes bibliographical references.
  1. Civil service—United States—States—Labor
productivity.   2. Local government—United States.
I. Title.
JK2465.C63   1976   331.1'18   76-2408
ISBN 0-87186-760-5   lib. bdg.
ISBN 0-87186-060-0   pbk.

First printing: March 1976
Second printing: April 1976
Third printing: April 1977
Paperbound: $2.50
Library binding: $4.00
Printed in the United States of America by Latham Process
  Corporation
Design: Harry Carter

COMMITTEE FOR ECONOMIC DEVELOPMENT
477 Madison Avenue, New York, N.Y. 10022

Contents

Responsibility for CED Statements on National Policy

The Committee for Economic Development is an independent research and educational organization of two hundred business executives and educators. CED is nonprofit, nonpartisan, and nonpolitical. Its purpose is to propose policies that will help to bring about steady economic growth at high employment and reasonably stable prices, increase productivity and living standards, provide greater and more equal opportunity for every citizen, and improve the quality of life for all. A more complete description of the objectives and organization of CED is to be found in the section beginning on page 92.

All CED policy recommendations must have the approval of the Research and Policy Committee, a group of sixty trustees whose names are listed on these pages. This Committee is directed under the bylaws to "initiate studies into the principles of business policy and of public policy which will foster the full contribution by industry and commerce to the attainment and maintenance" of the objectives stated above. The bylaws emphasize that "all research is to be thoroughly objective in character, and the approach in each instance is to be from the standpoint of the general welfare and not from that of any special political or economic group." The Committee is aided by a Research Advisory Board of leading social scientists and by a small permanent professional staff.

This statement by the Research and Policy Committee defines the dimensions of state and local government productivity, identifies the prin-

4

cipal areas of opportunity for improvement, outlines approaches that can motivate states and community jurisdictions to take action, and proposes steps that the states and the federal government can take to encourage productivity in the governments within their purview. The Committee is not attempting to pass judgment on any pending specific legislative proposals; its purpose is to urge careful consideration of the objectives set forth in the statement and of the best means of accomplishing those objectives.

Each statement on national policy is preceded by discussions, meetings, and exchanges of memoranda, often stretching over many months. The research is undertaken by a subcommittee, assisted by advisors chosen for their competence in the field under study. The members and advisors of the Improving Productivity in Government Subcommittee, which prepared this statement, are listed on page 6.

The full Research and Policy Committee participates in the drafting of findings and recommendations. Likewise, the trustees on the drafting subcommittee vote to approve or disapprove a policy statement, and they share with the Research and Policy Committee the privilege of submitting individual comments for publication, as noted on this and the following page and on the appropriate page of the text of the statement.

Except for the members of the Research and Policy Committee and the responsible subcommittee, the recommendations presented herein are not necessarily endorsed by other trustees or by the advisors, contributors, staff members, or others associated with CED.

6

Purpose of This Statement

STATE AND LOCAL GOVERNMENTS are a fundamental and integral part of our nation's overall economic well-being. Few realize that states and localities, not the federal government, are now primarily responsible for administering most of the tax dollars used to deliver public services. State and local spending accounts for over 80 percent of all nondefense government purchases of goods and services and almost 15 percent of the gross national product; together, these governments employ one of every seven non-agricultural workers.

Persistent inflation, compounded by an onerous recession, has intensified public concern with the cost and performance of government and has threatened the ability of even the most affluent jurisdictions to continue to function and fulfill their obligations. Yet, neither drastic cuts in spending in response to simplistic attacks on "big government" nor wholesale enlargements of public programs will meet the tough challenge of making government more productive and more responsive to genuine public needs.

Our report is not a direct response to some of the serious economic problems confronting state and local governments; its proposals are not calculated to provide the solution to immediate financial crises or the basis for a strengthened revenue structure. But in stressing the need for a wiser allocation and management of resources, this policy statement establishes many of the preconditions for restoring governments to a firmer financial footing.

Public Confidence. Revelations of public scandals and government mismanagement have added still another dimension to the importance of improved government productivity. By encouraging states and localities to identify needs, define their missions, and deliver services efficiently and effectively, we believe this statement will stimulate actions that can strengthen the credibility of public leadership and respect for public institutions at every level of government.

Even though it is gradually being recognized as an alternative to service cutbacks or higher taxes, productivity has remained a narrowly defined last-resort approach to specific problems. Too often, successful efforts are neither widely known nor readily available to other jurisdictions that could benefit from the experience. Beyond explaining the urgency of productivity, we intend this report to serve as a catalyst for productivity improvement through careful planning, effective management, and mobilization of the political desire to act.

Broadened Concept. Productivity in government encompasses a wide range of complicated and often controversial issues. In this statement, we seek to expand the awareness and understanding of productivity in a way that will give it prominence on the agenda of elected officials, public administrators, and citizens.

Our statement broadens the concept of productivity beyond its traditional definition. It is not enough to consider productivity a measure of output to input for a specific government activity or a limited means of either "getting more for less" or simply prompting bureaucrats to work harder. Productivity begins with a determination of goals and objectives (specifying what the government should and should not do) and then proceeds to identify the most cost-effective means of achieving those ends. Only after these two fundamental steps have been taken will improvement in efficiency (the traditional ratio of resources to results) be significant and meaningful.

Four Areas of Opportunity. Numerous factors, individually and in relation to one another, affect productivity. In this report, we identify four main areas of opportunity: strengthening management, motivating the work force, improving technology and increasing capital investment, and measuring both immediate results and the full impact of government programs. We also explain closely related activities needed to start and to sustain productivity improvement, including the provision of formal systems of evaluation, the introduction of competition and consumer choice, and the encouragement of political support for productivity programs. Although we recognize the unique character of government, we nevertheless believe that many of the principles used in private enterprise can be applied in the public sector.

With 50 states and some 39,000 general-purpose governments, it would have been impossible to outline specific actions that would apply equally to a Los Angeles and a Peoria. Therefore, we identify the principal deficiencies and opportunities for improvement that are common to most state and local jurisdictions, and we suggest general approaches that they can adapt to their particular circumstances. Our specific recommendations (summarized in Chapter 1 and discussed in detail in Chapter 5) show how states and the federal government can encourage and assist jurisdictions within their purview to adopt methods of operation that will lead to productivity improvement.

Improving Productivity in State and Local Government continues CED's work in the field of improving the management of government. Our direct interest in productivity stems from CED's studies of education, welfare, health care, and other services; we found states and localities lagging behind other sectors of the economy in the management of these functions. Our statements *Modernizing Local Government* (1966), *Modernizing State Government* (1967), and *Reshaping Government in Metropolitan Areas* (1970) focused on the need for strong structural, financial, legal, and administrative foundations to provide effective and efficient state and local government. This report builds on that base by explaining how these governments can better transform tax dollars into services that actually meet citizen needs. An in-depth examination of labor relations and employee compensation will be made in a subsequent project.

Acknowledgments. The subcommittee that prepared this report included a number of trustees with experience in government as well as an impressive panel of advisors from the academic community and public policy study groups. A list of subcommittee members appears on page 6. I acknowledge particularly the contributions of the chairman, Wayne E. Thompson, senior vice president of the Dayton Hudson Corporation, Minneapolis, who served as city manager of both Richmond and Oakland, California, and Rocco C. Siciliano, chairman of the TI Corporation, Los Angeles, who has been an undersecretary of commerce and an assistant secretary of labor. R. Scott Fosler, project director and director of government studies at CED, deserves special recognition for bringing a fresh and constructive approach to this most perplexing and difficult problem and for his skilled preparation of this report.

Philip M. Klutznick, *Chairman*
Research and Policy Committee

Introduction and Summary
of Recommendations

IN STATES AND COMMUNITIES across the nation, elected officials are telling their constituents that soaring costs confront government with two alternatives: either increase taxes or cut back services. Many governments today are doing both. Only a few farsighted leaders have broken away from this conventional response to pose a third option: that more intelligent use be made of existing resources to achieve desired goals; that is, increase government productivity.*

Many Americans continue to harbor an image of state and local government as a community housekeeper or overhead operation required to support the more productive elements of the economy. But the facts are otherwise. The services provided by states and localities—education, law enforcement, fire protection, social services, health care, public works, environmental improvement, and numerous others—are fundamentally important in their own right, especially because they directly affect the quality of American life.

The resources consumed to produce these services have grown to a magnitude that makes state and local government one of the major components of the American economy. From 1954 to 1974, state and local purchases of goods and services grew almost sevenfold, from $27 billion to $192 billion; more significantly, that spending increased from 7.4 to 13.7 percent of the gross national product. (See Figure 1, page 13.) During the

*See memorandum by FRANKLIN A. LINDSAY, page 79.

same period, the number of state and local employees increased from 4.6 million to 11.6 million persons, or to about 1 in 7 nonagricultural workers in the United States.

Productivity growth in the private sector has sustained America's high standard of living and opportunity. Private-sector productivity averaged about 2.5 percent annually from 1900 to 1947; since then, it has grown by an average of 3 percent a year. Although the rate of productivity growth began to slow in the late 1960s, hourly production per worker is still four times what it was a half century ago.

But Americans can no longer look solely to the private sector for productivity increases that will improve economic well-being. Given the shift in national resources to state and local governments and the significance of the services they provide, we must look there, as well, for greater productivity.

Previous CED statements on modernizing state, local, and metropolitan government focused on the structural foundations required for effective and efficient government. Such foundations, including the creation of regional institutions, improved community-level government within metropolitan areas, and the provision of modern organizational structures and administrative machinery, are critical to more productive government, but they are not sufficient. This statement probes still deeper into the process by which governments actually transform resources into services that meet public needs.

Improving government productivity is not a quick solution to imminent financial problems or an antidote to a weak tax base. It is a long-term task that requires continuing attention to every phase of government operations. There is no single correct approach. Efforts to improve government productivity must recognize the interplay between political forces and agency operations, between broad policy considerations and detailed administrative matters, between technology and people, between analytic technique and bureaucratic behavior, and between local prerogatives and national responsibilities.

This statement is an overview that identifies and links together the numerous elements that bear on government productivity so that more effective and coordinated action can be taken toward improvement. Its purposes are to define the dimensions of state and local government productivity, to identify the principal opportunities for improvement, to determine approaches for strengthening the forces that can motivate government, and to suggest how the federal system can encourage and assist states and localities in getting on with the task.

Figure 1: GOVERNMENT PURCHASES OF GOODS AND SERVICES
IN THE UNITED STATES, 1954 AND 1974[a]

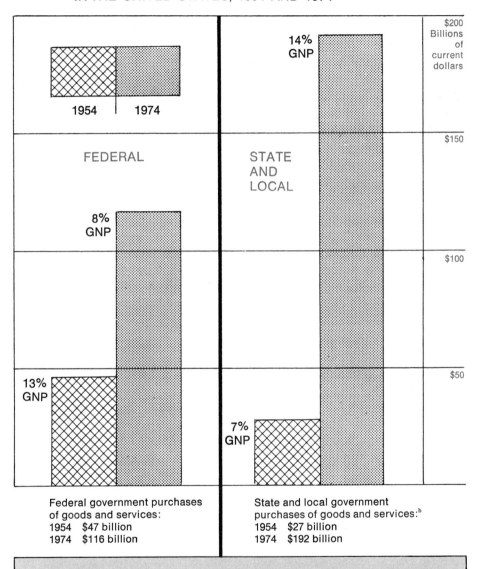

Federal government purchases
of goods and services:
1954 $47 billion
1974 $116 billion

State and local government
purchases of goods and services:[b]
1954 $27 billion
1974 $192 billion

[a] Excludes transfer payments to individuals (social security, welfare, and so forth), which increased from $15 billion, or 4 percent of GNP, in 1954 to $134 billion, or 9.6 percent of GNP, in 1974.
[b] Total includes purchases made with federal grants.
Source: *Economic Report of the President* (Washington, D.C.: U.S. Government Printing Office, February 1975).

Because we recognize that governments vary widely in structure, legal constraints, size, and population served, we have not attempted to make specific recommendations that would be applicable to the great diversity of jurisdictions in the United States. Rather, we have identified the principal areas of opportunity for improving productivity and have underscored the responsibility of each government and the citizens it serves to take the initiative to exploit those opportunities as applicable to its jurisdiction. Our more specific recommendations focus on steps that can be taken by the states and the federal government to encourage and assist productivity improvement in the governments within their purview. Those recommendations are summarized here and elaborated in Chapter 5.

We are mindful of the political impediments to many of the approaches we suggest. However, most of the important changes in state and local government, such as use of city managers and establishment of metropolitan institutions, had to overcome formidable resistance where they have been adopted. Productivity is different from such changes in that it is not a technique or specific innovation but rather a concept or way of doing business that stresses higher overall performance at minimum cost. It is our hope that emphasis on improving productivity will become an integral goal of state and local politics and government operations.

MEANING OF PRODUCTIVITY IN GOVERNMENT

The concept of productivity implies a ratio of the quantity and/or quality of results (output) to the resources (input) invested to achieve them. Government productivity has two dimensions: effectiveness and efficiency.

Effectiveness concerns the extent to which government programs achieve their objectives. This presumes that decisions about what and how much governments do are based on considered judgments of the relative importance and cost of meeting public needs. Perceptions of need, in turn, are presumably based on demands and expectations of voters and consumers as expressed through the political process.*

Efficiency concerns the organization of resources to carry out government programs and functions at minimal cost. Efficiency may be expressed in several ways, including output per manhour, capital-output ratios, and more broadly, least-cost combinations of resources.

*See memorandum by CHARLES P. BOWEN, JR., page 79.

Productivity improvement, therefore, is an increase in the ratio of outputs to inputs, that is, providing more effective or higher-quality services at the same cost (or the same services at lower cost).

The inputs to government are relatively easy to define. They are the goods and services purchased by government from individuals (mainly public employees) and from outside organizations (mainly private firms). They can be measured in conventional terms: manhours, machine time, or money costs per unit. (The definition becomes more complex if one includes the contribution of the service consumer, for example, the ability and motivation of a student, or the environment in which the service is performed, for example, the classroom and the backgrounds of pupils.)

The outputs or results of government activity are more difficult to define. Some government services, such as refuse collection, are similar to those provided in the private sector; but because they are financed primarily by taxes, their objectives or value cannot be readily determined by market criteria, as in business. Government activities that aim to achieve broad social goals, such as creating a sense of physical security, are more difficult to define. In such instances, it is important to consider the full impact and consequences of government actions rather than just outputs, which refer to the immediate results of program activity. An added complication in defining outputs is that the services provided by public agencies are of less interest to some political groups than the inputs themselves; those who compete for government jobs, contracts, prestigious positions, and political power thus come into conflict with consumers and taxpayers who want quality public services at lower costs.

However, to discard the economic distinction between inputs and outputs would be to give equal weight to all political objectives, no matter how narrow or self-serving, thus abandoning any concept of the public interest and any hope of improving or even defining government's contribution to the quality of life. Although government serves many functions in addition to providing services (including promoting equality and resolving political differences),[1] for the purpose of defining and improving productivity, we view government outputs in the narrow economic sense: as those goods and services that governments produce for consumers.

1/A recent study by a group of municipal officials assessed the various roles of local government in light of the need for improved productivity. See Maryland Municipal League, *The Challenge to Municipal Government* (Annapolis, 1974).

THREE STEPS TOWARD GREATER PRODUCTIVITY

Government productivity requires attention to each of three steps in the process of transforming public desires and tax money into accomplishments: identifying goals and objectives, choosing among alternative approaches to achieve objectives, and implementing programs.

Identifying Goals and Objectives.* Productivity must first be concerned with what government should or should not be doing to meet citizens' needs and desires. In theory, such determinations are made by collective choice through the elected representatives of the people. In practice, however, the political process rarely works so neatly.

Even in small towns with homogeneous populations, differences may exist between younger newcomers who opt for higher standards of education and older residents who may prefer more convenient transportation or better police protection. In larger jurisdictions, where there are widely diverse economic, racial, and ethnic groups, collective choice is an even more dubious concept.

In most jurisdictions, small but effective citizens' groups actively appeal to elected officials and government agencies for new programs or increased budget allocations for existing programs (e.g., a swimming pool or a new library). Because they do not pay directly or totally for those services, which are financed mainly by taxes, such groups are rarely concerned about the cost of what they request.

Most citizens are poorly informed about what government does, have infrequent personal contact with government bureaucracy, and become concerned only when there are apparent breakdowns of crucial public services. Public perceptions of the quality of a government service may be quite at odds with what objective indicators reveal about that service.

In the absence of more objective criteria, elected officials are likely to establish or modify goals on the basis of demands from pressure groups, levels of complaints, their own political ambitions, and views expressed through the media, which both reflect and create public attitudes. Few public officials consider what their respective governments *ought* to be doing, focusing instead on the more immediate problems associated with what they *are* doing. Where questions of purpose and performance are raised, functional fragmentation permits responsibility to be passed from agency to agency. Thus, the police blame the courts for failure to punish criminal offenders; prosecutors claim that the police fail to supply evidence

*See memorandum by MARK SHEPHERD, JR., page 80.

needed for conviction; and all blame correctional institutions for not re-habilitating convicted felons.

Such behavior can be explained to some extent by the nebulous and conflicting nature of public goals. However, to excuse nonperformance by government agencies on the grounds that many of their goals and ob-jectives are intangible is to evade the primary issue. The ultimate objective of *most* activities, including those in the private business sector, are in-tangible. *With any activity, the essential priority is to devote continual attention to its major purpose, however difficult that may be to define. Intangible goals must be redefined in terms of more specific and tangible objectives that can be measured.* Only then can resources be allocated to-ward their accomplishment, strategies and activities planned and carried out, responsibility for actions assigned to specific people, and performance ultimately evaluated so that someone can be held accountable for results.

We are not suggesting that there are necessarily right or wrong politi-cal and social goals that can be set in perfect harmony. However, improve-ments can be made in identifying goals that more nearly reflect a syn-thesis and account for a range of community needs and desires, and in setting tangible objectives that will most readily lead to the attainment of those goals.

Choosing among Alternatives. In order to achieve basic goals and objectives, choices should be made among alternative approaches. *Selection of approaches with the highest cost-effectiveness ratio presents the greatest opportunity for improving government productivity.* It also poses the most difficult problem of public management. How should housing be provided to low-income families: through government-con-structed housing, rent supplements, or general income-maintenance pro-grams? Which approach will more effectively hold down crime rates: increasing the certainty of apprehension, conviction, and punishment of offenders or providing job opportunities for unemployed teen-agers, who commit a disproportionate amount of crime?

In practice, few jurisdictions systematically identify policy alterna-tives, let alone analyze their relative costs and benefits. Rather, agencies tend to persist in using time-honored if demonstrably ineffective ap-proaches and techniques simply because they do not know of better means or have no incentive to seek alternatives. Government agencies thus miss opportunities both for improved achievement and for cost savings that can be realized by eliminating marginally useful activities. The unexamined life, said Socrates, is not worth living; in government, the unexamined program is frequently not worth maintaining.

Implementation: The Business of Getting Things Done. *The time-tested principles of organization, specialization, supervision, communication, and established procedures are still largely valid; the missing ingredient in many government agencies has been the will and ability of managers to apply them.*

Many government operations, however, have become so large and complex that they require more sophisticated techniques of analysis, technological application, and management skill than those traditionally used by most governments. The problems of implementing government policy are currently little understood, involving as they do nebulous and often conflicting objectives, interaction among numerous government and non-government groups, and the need to balance political with technical considerations. Policy guidance from top officials is often so broad and ambiguous (in some cases necessarily so) that it places great responsibility for policy making in the hands of lower-level administrators. In turn, policy implementation in key functions rests heavily with the individual employee (the policeman, teacher, social worker, and others) who actually delivers the service or otherwise represents government to the public. Management in many government operations is less a matter of issuing directives from central command posts and more a process of communication and persuasion among top management, middle-level supervisors, employees, and citizen-consumers.

PROGRESS TOWARD IMPROVEMENT

Only very crude estimates of overall state and local government productivity are possible with the data now available. Although some jurisdictions have made significant progress, existing data suggest that productivity may have declined in other areas. There are great disparities in performance levels from city to city; for example, one city collects three times as much refuse per manhour as another of similar size and topography. The absence of comparable performance data itself suggests lack of interest in productivity on the part of local officials. The federal government has undertaken a major effort to measure its own output and reports that the 65 percent of the federal civilian work force whose performance can be measured quantitatively improved their productivity by an average of 1.5 percent annually from 1967 to 1974.[2] This effort under-scores the potential both for measuring and for improving government productivity.

Some governments are paying greater attention to analyzing program benefits and costs and ways to improve and reduce the costs of operations in refuse collection, health care, police services, and other functions. A few states have created machinery to handle metropolitan-wide problems in a number of areas. Several states and localities have developed out-standing records for effective management. Such achievements can provide the momentum for further progress.

But the effort to date has been small in comparison with the need. Many state and local governments have been slow to recognize that a new era of problems and opportunities is upon them. In 1966, CED's policy statement *Modernizing Local Government* described a lack of motivation and capability that is still characteristic of too many of the nation's local governments. Some simply fail to perceive the creative and energetic efforts of other states and localities and will find they are being rapidly outpaced; others watch the new developments with indifference and skep-ticism.

The responsibility for lack of interest in productivity at the state and local levels lies in large measure with the public (business, labor, the media, and individual citizens). In the end, government responds to what voters and citizens demand of it. More effective and efficient govern-ment seems to be a topic a little on everybody's mind but not much on anybody's agenda. There is no cohesive constituency to push for it, as there are powerful constituencies that fight for more services and subsidies, higher wages, and larger contracts.

PRINCIPAL AREAS OF OPPORTUNITY

Despite the diversity of America's 39,000 states, counties, townships, and municipalities, certain deficiencies and opportunities for improvement can be identified that are common to a large proportion of their govern-ments.

2/Joint Financial Management Improvement Program, *Annual Report to the President and the Congress: Productivity Programs in the Federal Government FY 1974*, vol. 1, *Current Efforts and Future Prospects* (Washington, D.C., June 1975).

Strengthened Management. *The greatest opportunity for improved government productivity lies in strengthened management.* Deficiencies in management derive largely from the absence of political pressure for productivity on top elected officials (governors, mayors, county executives, legislatures, and councils) and from the failure to link the performance of agencies directly to the salaries and promotions of responsible managers.

Improvements can be made in each of the three principal elements of government management: planning and budgeting, decision making, and operations. More effective recruitment and development of government managers are also required.

Work Force. The potential of employees, which is critical to productivity because government operations are labor-intensive, has not been fully developed. This statement does not attempt a detailed examination of worker motivation and labor relations because these will be subjects of a future policy statement. However, three issues of prime concern should be mentioned here.

First, collective bargaining is changing the relationship between public managers and employees, raising important questions about the political strength of labor in determining settlements and changing the climate of management through the blurring of distinctions between negotiable labor concerns and basic management prerogatives. The practices and traditions that are established now will determine for years to come whether collective bargaining will enhance or impede government productivity.

Second, many civil service systems show signs of rigidities and other tendencies that impede productivity.

Third, changes in the education, skills, and attitudes of workers require managers to rethink traditional modes of operation and personnel management, especially in those functions that require a high degree of employee discretion in carrying out policy.

Technology and Capital Investment. Much of the gain in productivity in industry has resulted from technological advances and capital investment. Numerous examples of innovation in cities, counties, and states (in better refuse collection devices, new fire fighting apparatus, and improved police communication equipment) have demonstrated that ingenuity, experimentation, and perseverance can produce results in the public sector as well. *We believe that greater use of technology will depend* *largely upon the demand created for it by state and local governments through better identification and communication of need to potential suppliers, a more aggressive search for existing technologies, and the appropriation of funds explicitly for technological screening, experimentation, and implementation.*

Improved Measurement. *State and local governments should improve the measurement of their activities by employing existing but little-used techniques that provide basic management information and by developing and adopting newer techniques that focus on the evaluation of results.* The indicators should focus on social conditions, program effectiveness, and program efficiency. When coupled with political and professional judgment and assessed against costs, a combination of indicators can provide a more complete understanding of the overall productivity of most government activities.

FORCES FOR
MOTIVATING GOVERNMENT

Quality government ultimately depends upon the political demand for it. There is no single formula for producing the political pressure for productivity that is required to motivate elected officials. This is the responsibility of citizens under our democratic form of government. Nevertheless, the perceptions and reactions of voters combine with and are influenced by a number of other external forces that bear on the administration of public programs.

Mechanisms for Evaluation. *Audit agencies should follow the example of the U.S. General Accounting Office in concentrating increasingly on the effectiveness of government programs and the efficiency with which they are carried out, rather than just on financial administration and legislative compliance.*

Beyond an expanded audit role, however, high-level organizations with public prestige and visibility are needed to assess independently the performance of state and local governments. Such organizations would require regular and independent sources of financing to support a professional staff for analyzing services and mobilizing public support for improvement.

Promoting Competition and Consumer Choice. The monopolistic character of most public-service agencies is one reason for their lack of interest in productivity. *One way of responding to this situation is to encourage competition and consumer choice.* Under some circumstances, governments can achieve better performance by contracting with either public agencies or private organizations for services. Competition can be enhanced by supplying consumers with vouchers or other forms of purchasing power and permitting them to select services from private or public suppliers; fostering competition among government agencies, where this is feasible, can extend consumer choice.

Political Impetus and Support from Outside Groups. *Sustained improvement will require action by groups that can bring pressure to bear on government or otherwise offer support and expertise that can improve productivity.* Such groups include public-interest and government-reform groups; business, which can provide technical assistance in areas of government akin to business operations as well as increase its involvement in public affairs; both public and private organized labor, which is in a key position to identify opportunities for improving productivity (private unions can also bring pressure to bear on public unions to recognize the importance of productivity improvement); the media, which is the public's principal source of information on government operations; political parties, which at present have much to gain from demonstrating genuine concern for the ability of government to deliver on promises without adding to the tax burden; and educational institutions, particularly in providing training and direct technical assistance to states and localities.

RESPONSIBILITIES IN THE FEDERAL SYSTEM

The principal responsibility for exploiting the opportunities for improving productivity rests with the states and localities themselves and with the citizens they serve.* Nevertheless, state and local governments function as a part of the federal system, which can operate either to impede or to assist their efforts toward improvement.*

State Role. Building upon their traditional responsibilities for establishing the foundations for effective local government, states have a central role in providing leadership, incentives, and technical assistance for raising

*See memoranda by OSCAR A. LUNDIN, page 80.

the productivity of their local governments and for removing the numerous state-imposed impediments to more effective internal management.

A long-overdue action by the states is to overhaul the structure of local government. **We recommend that state governments move vigorously to improve the structure of local government. Such measures should include the creation of regional, metropolitan, local, and neighborhood institutions; the redefinition or redistribution of government powers and functions; and the authorization to permit local units to utilize intergovernmental contracting and other cooperative service arrangements.***

States can also encourage the employment of professionally trained administrators. **We recommend that state governments encourage and assist smaller governments in enlisting professional management (such as the circuit city manager or other manpower-pooling arrangements) and larger units in providing management training for top administrators and creating full-time administrative units staffed by personnel professionally trained in management and analysis.**

Mobility of personnel should be encouraged so that professional skills will be used where they are most needed. **We recommend that state and local government personnel systems be modified to allow employees to move among local and state agencies without loss of rank, seniority, or pension rights.***

A basic impediment to improved productivity is the absence of information by which performance can be evaluated by local governments themselves and by nongovernment groups. **We recommend that state governments establish and enforce minimum standards for local government budgeting, accounting, and performance and reporting systems that would provide data on the level, quality, results, and costs of services.***

State and local governments lack mechanisms for systematically evaluating performance and taking action to encourage and assist local governments in improvement. In choosing among the available options, careful consideration should be given to selecting those approaches that are most appropriate for the diverse government systems in the various states. **We recommend that the governor of each state establish a high-level commission with state, local, and nongovernment representation to identify and suggest the creation of permanent mechanisms for evaluating and improving state and local government productivity.** Options to be considered include expansion of the traditional audit function to include performance reporting and evaluation, creation of an agency in the executive office of the governor (or assignment to another state agency) with responsibility for periodically evaluating and assisting in the improvement

*See memoranda by FRAZAR B. WILDE, page 81.

of local government productivity, and creation of a nongovernmental quasi-public institution with high visibility and a professional staff for the evaluation of state and local governments.

State governments should also provide financial and technical assistance to local governments for the purposes of developing and implementing performance measures, experimenting with or implementing techniques or programs that have the greatest likelihood of success, and undertaking other programs that would improve productivity.

Federal Action. The federal government also has a role to play in improving the productivity of state and local governments.

Restructuring federal assistance. The current spectrum of federal assistance programs to states and localities, ranging from general revenue sharing with few administrative requirements to categorical grants with detailed guidelines for implementation, fails to use federal influence to improve state and local government productivity and in some ways actually impedes productivity. **We recommend that federal grants, including revenue sharing, block grants, and categorical programs, be redesigned to encourage improvements in the structure and internal management of state and local governments that will enhance productivity.*** There are several options by which federal grants could help to increase the capacity of states and localities to determine their own needs, to choose among alternative approaches, and to implement programs. These include:

Requiring that grant recipients meet specified administrative criteria**

Requiring that a specific percentage of federal grants be expended for the development and implementation of techniques to measure, analyze, and improve operations

Establishing bonus payments for those states and localities that meet specified administrative requirements or develop and implement their own programs for measuring, analyzing, and improving operations

For categorical programs specifically, placing greater emphasis on achieving program objectives and quality performance and less stress on guidelines and requirements for program implementation

However, higher administrative standards do not address the more complex problems of managing government. **We recommend that federal financial and technical assistance to state and local governments for improving internal management be expanded.**

The modification of federal assistance to encourage productivity improvement is a continuing task that needs to be coordinated at the federal level by a management-oriented agency. **We recommend that the President designate a federal agency to develop policy and coordinate implementation of federal assistance to states and localities with the participation of state and local officials. This agency should have direct access to the chief executive.***

Improving public-sector manpower policy. In addition to using the power of federal grants to improve productivity, steps could be taken to encourage more effective use of professional personnel to strengthen public-sector management. **We recommend that the Intergovernmental Personnel Act (IPA) programs of interchange among federal, state, and local governments be expanded and, in addition, that interchanges between the private and public sectors be promoted. We further recommend that the U.S. Civil Service Commission's Bureau of Intergovernmental Personnel Programs or the National Commission for Manpower Policy undertake a major review of public-sector manpower policy in order to determine ways to make state and local civil service and personnel systems more conducive to productivity improvement and to examine possibilities for nationwide mechanisms of recruitment, interchange, and pension portability for state and local personnel.**

More effective innovation, research, and development. To date, federal research and development has been deficient in strengthening state and local government. Too little of the overall federal effort has focused on state and local needs; there has been a tendency to apply research and experimentation randomly, with a consequent diffusion of effort; and dissemination of results has been inadequate. **We recommend that federally sponsored research and development be restructured to devote a larger share of resources to problems facing state and local governments in a way that would involve state and local officials in identifying priorities and approaches, emphasizing systematic experimentation, and improving the dissemination of results.**

Leadership for improvement. Success in improving state and local government productivity will require strong and effective national leadership, not to propose pat solutions that would be futile given the diversity of America's government jurisdictions, but to provide the stimulation, imagination, and resources required for mounting a long-term effort that encourages state and local actions toward improvement. **We recommend**

that the President and Congress demonstrate their concern for improving state and local government productivity through support of an effective federal effort to provide leadership, coordination among federal agencies, and involvement and stimulation of state and local governments. We applaud the conversion of the National Commission on Productivity and Work Quality into the permanent National Center for Productivity and Quality of Working Life. However, to be effective, the new center requires funding substantially beyond its current annual appropriation of $2 million.*

Our concern for greater productivity arose initially from the realization that state and local governments were consuming an ever greater share of national resources without demonstrable improvements in services, thereby constituting a potential source of inflation and a drag on the economy. That concern persists. But the importance of improving productivity goes beyond the issue of cost and even beyond the desirability of achieving higher quality and effectiveness in the important services that government provides. It goes directly to the need for restoring confidence in government.

We are not suggesting that improving state and local productivity is all that is required to restore national confidence in government. The highest priority is the demonstration of integrity and decency by public institutions. However, full confidence will be established only when the nation is also reassured of the competence of government. We believe that a practical way to contribute to that objective is to strengthen the capacity of states and localities to deliver quality public services at reasonable cost.

For the past forty years, ideas and energy for improving government have flowed principally from the national to the local level. We believe that the time has come to stimulate a flow in the opposite direction by generating in communities across the nation the ability to manage their affairs effectively and creatively. In this way, the nation as a whole can draw upon the models of excellence that hold promise for improving the productivity of the public sector.

We are encouraged by some signs of vitality and imagination that are clearly visible and growing at the state and local levels. We are dismayed by the slowness of progress and the resistance of many governments to necessary change. Above all, we are convinced that the potential for improving the productivity of state and local government is great and waiting to be tapped.

*See memorandum by R. HEATH LARRY, page 83.

Reasons for Concern

THE SLACKENING OF AMERICAN PRODUCTIVITY GROWTH in the late sixties prompted the President to create the National Commission on Productivity[1] to inquire into causes and possible solutions. The commission identified numerous reasons for lagging productivity and concluded that there were three broad areas of opportunity for improvement: use of human resources, technology and capital investment, and impact of government regulation on business. The commission also noted the rapid increase in the size of the public sector as a possible factor in slowing overall productivity and concluded that many of the means used to improve productivity in industry may be applicable to government as well.

A grave deficiency in assessing public-sector productivity is the absence of measures of most government output. Public-sector output, as calculated in GNP, does not directly reflect goods and services produced and delivered; rather, it is the cost of goods and services purchased by governments. This measure is employed because it is claimed that most of the things governments produce cannot readily be quantified. The private

---

1/The commission was subsequently renamed the National Commission on Productivity and Work Quality and in December 1975 was converted into the National Center for Productivity and Quality of Working Life.

sector encounters similar difficulty in quantifying service output but can determine the value of services as registered in consumer purchases. The federal effort to measure and improve the productivity of federal agencies (noted in Chapter 1) at least partly counters the contention that government productivity can be neither measured nor improved.

At the state and local levels, however, the situation is cloudier. There is little clear evidence that productivity in state and local government has kept pace with productivity in the private sector, and there are reasons to raise the possibility that productivity in some activities or jurisdictions may have been falling. This is an especially dim prospect given the growing importance of state and local government, where expansion has exceeded that of any other economic sector.

GROWTH OF GOVERNMENT IN
THE NATIONAL ECONOMY

Overall government activity in the United States has expanded in terms of both expenditures and number of employees.

Expenditures. Government expenditures consist of purchases of goods and services (which are the resources employed in the production and delivery of public services and which serve as a proxy for final results in measuring GNP) and transfers to persons (which consist mainly of social security and public assistance and related payments).

The rise in public expenditures from 1954 to 1974 (shown in Figure 2, page 29) reveals several important shifts in the quantitative importance of government in the economy.

Government expenditures rose from 27 percent of GNP in 1954 to 33 percent in 1974. The overall rise, however, was chiefly a result of an increase in transfer payments to persons from 4 percent to nearly 10 percent.

Government purchases of goods and services as a proportion of GNP increased only slightly, from 20 to 22 percent. However, the proportion accounted for by the federal government fell sharply, from 13 to 8 percent (mainly the result of a decline in the relative weight of defense expenditures); whereas the state and local proportion rose sharply, from about 7 to 14 percent.

State and local governments accounted for more than 80 percent of total government purchases of goods and services for nondefense purposes

Figure 2: PUBLIC EXPENDITURES IN THE UNITED STATES AS
PERCENT OF GNP, 1954 AND 1974 (billions)[a]

	Amount[a]		Percent of GNP	
	1954	1974	1954	1974
GNP	$365	$1,397	100.0	100.0
Total government expenditures[b]	97	461	26.6	33.0
Federal	70	299	19.2	21.4
State and local	30	206	8.2	14.7
Components of federal expenditures[c]				
Purchases of goods and services	47	116	12.9	8.3
Defense	41	79	11.2	5.7
Nondefense	6	38	1.6	2.7
Transfers to persons	12	114	3.3	8.2
Grants to state and local governments	3	44	0.8	3.1
Components of state and local expenditures[c]				
Purchases of goods and services	27	192	7.4	13.7
Transfers to persons	3	20	0.8	1.4

[a] Expressed in current dollars.
[b] Federal grants to state and local governments are included in the federal and the state and local expenditures, but the duplication is eliminated in the combined total.
[c] Omits several miscellaneous items.
Source: *Economic Report of the President* (Washington, D.C.: U.S. Government Printing Office, February 1975).

at both the beginning and the end of the period. It is the states and localities that are principally responsible for transforming tax dollars into domestic public services, not the federal government, as is commonly believed.

Employment. Data on government employment tell the same story. In 1974, governments of all kinds employed 14.3 million civilians, or 18 percent of workers in nonagricultural establishments in the United States. Eighty-one percent were state and local; 19 percent were federal. As Figure 3 (page 31) indicates, the increase in state and local government employment during the 1954–1974 period was nearly seven times that of the federal government and three times that of the private sector.

REASONS FOR THE RISE IN
THE COST OF STATE AND LOCAL GOVERNMENT

The almost sevenfold increase in state and local government expenditures between 1954 and 1974 was attributable to both an expansion of activity and an increase in the unit cost of goods and services purchased by government.

Expansion of State and Local Activity. Several factors contributed to this expansion.

There has simply been an increase in the number of people to be served. The total population rose by 31 percent, and the number of people living in urban areas (where demands for government services are highest) rose by some 48 percent.

The workload in traditional government services was increased by urban growth and its concomitants, such as increases in the number of automobiles, amounts of solid waste, and commission of crime. The postwar baby boom, in particular, created a wave of demand for education that moved from primary and secondary schools to colleges.

Rising affluence enabled governments to establish higher levels of service in existing functions. In education, for example, these took the form of foreign language training in elementary schools, preschool programs, remedial reading programs, and more teaching assistants. The demand for higher levels of service has been reinforced on the supply side by the tendency of some professional bureaucracies to increase service activities in

Figure 3: GOVERNMENT AND PRIVATE EMPLOYMENT
IN THE UNITED STATES, 1954 AND 1974[a] (millions)

	1954	1974	Percent Increase
Federal government	2.2	2.7	22.7
State and local government	4.6	11.6	152.2
Private sector	42.3	64.0	51.3
Total nonagricultural employment	49.0	78.3	59.8

[a] Refers to wage and salary workers in nonagricultural establishments.
Source: *Economic Report of the President* (Washington, D.C.: U.S. Government Printing Office, February 1975).

health, mass transportation, recreation, housing, education, and other fields.

Transfer payments and other benefits to lower-income groups expanded to keep pace with rising living standards, inflation, and higher expectations of government services and benefits.

Finally, state and local government expanded into new fields, such as manpower development to provide special occupational training for young and older workers and pollution control and other environmental protection programs to meet emerging public needs and desires.

Figure 4 (page 33) presents a breakdown of expenditures on major government functions between 1954 and 1974. Education was by far the most costly function of state and local government, accounting for 34 percent of the total increase in costs.* Public welfare accounted for less than 12 percent of the total increase. Expenditures classified as "Other" include both utilities and a large number of activities that although less costly

*See memorandum by MARK SHEPHERD, JR., page 83.

can nevertheless have a significant impact on economic activity and the quality of life (e.g., planning, inspections, consumer affairs, landlord-tenant relations, and general government administration).

Increase in the Price of Inputs. In addition to the cost increase resulting from the growing volume of inputs, there was a rapid rise in the price paid for each unit of input. As Figure 5 (page 35) indicates, the rise in the price of a unit of input has been higher for state and local government than for any other economic sector. This results partially from increases in the price of goods and outside services purchased by government but principally from increased wages and fringe benefits for employees.

In the past twenty years, wage rates for state and local public employees have increased more rapidly than those of any other major employment group (see Figure 6, page 37). There are several reasons for this. Public employees' wages in some jurisdictions have been increased to achieve comparability with their counterparts in the private sector. The rapid expansion in public employment during the 1950s and 1960s led to higher salaries to attract labor from other sectors. The number of professional and technical positions in higher salary brackets increased. Public employees have been rapidly unionizing and increasing their economic and political strength.

Employee compensation also includes fringe benefits. Expenditures for pensions alone totaled $5.9 billion in 1974, representing about 6 percent of total compensation to state and local government employees.[2] Those pension systems that are not fully funded face rapid cost increases in the future. Other benefits, including medical and life insurance, may be nearly equivalent to pension costs. If vacations and other compensated days off are counted, the total fringe benefit package represents a significantly higher proportion of total employee compensation.

Overall, the increase in the unit cost of state and local purchases was 152 percent from 1954 to 1974, compared with an 83 percent rise in consumer prices. Although this figure indicates how much more governments paid for a unit of input, it does not explain how much more was paid for a unit of public service because there is no overall measure of government output.

2/"Social Welfare Expenditures, Fiscal Year 1974," *Social Security Bulletin,* January 1975, page 8.

Figure 4: STATE AND LOCAL GOVERNMENT EXPENDITURES,
SELECTED FUNCTIONS, 1954 AND 1974 (millions)

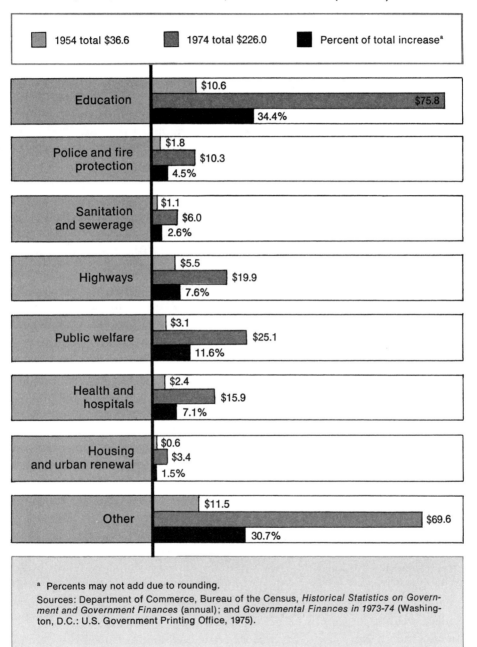

1954 total $36.6   1974 total $226.0   Percent of total increase[a]

Education
$10.6
$75.8
34.4%

Police and fire protection
$1.8
$10.3
4.5%

Sanitation and sewerage
$1.1
$6.0
2.6%

Highways
$5.5
$19.9
7.6%

Public welfare
$3.1
$25.1
11.6%

Health and hospitals
$2.4
$15.9
7.1%

Housing and urban renewal
$0.6
$3.4
1.5%

Other
$11.5
$69.6
30.7%

[a] Percents may not add due to rounding.

Sources: Department of Commerce, Bureau of the Census, *Historical Statistics on Government and Government Finances* (annual); and *Governmental Finances in 1973-74* (Washington, D.C.: U.S. Government Printing Office, 1975).

STRAIN ON STATE AND LOCAL REVENUE

To pay their rising costs, both state and local governments have increased their tax rates sharply. The ratio of state and local tax and nontax revenues (excluding federal grants-in-aid) to personal income rose from 8.9 percent in 1954 to 14.3 percent in 1974. In many areas, especially big cities with large poverty populations and shaky economies, the proportions were much higher. New York City's general expenditures, for example, were about 22.6 percent of its personal income in 1973. The strain is all the greater because state and local government revenues are less responsive than federal taxes to increases in income.

Tax increases are one of the most sensitive issues of state and local politics. Nevertheless, as long as rising national incomes could support both expanding levels of consumption per household and more costly state and local services, taxpayer protests remained within political bounds. In essence, taxpayers either desired or acquiesced in the diversion of more of their purchasing power to state and local government. However, with the decline in the purchasing power of after-tax consumer incomes that began in the early 1970s, taxpayer protests and revolts mounted to levels unprecedented in the postwar period. Faced with slackening or falling revenues, growing taxpayer resistance to higher taxes, and higher interest rates for municipal bonds, government administrators everywhere have been forced to look for ways to close the gap between revenues and expenditures.

Generally, the first response of government officials to these pressures is to find additional revenues. However, their efforts have been frustrated on all fronts. Not only do taxpayers resist higher tax rates, but increased taxes also entail the risk of driving middle- and upper-income residents and businesses out of hard-pressed jurisdictions, thereby further eroding the tax base. States are reluctant to expand local taxing authority. Both states and the federal government resist increases in grant assistance. Local officials are limited in their ability to strengthen the local tax base as a means of increasing revenue (although there is potential for more effective action by local governments to strengthen their economic activity). And although a full-employment economy would increase state and local revenues by an estimated $25 to $30 billion, the tools to stimulate general economic growth lie almost exclusively with the federal government. Finally, New York City's fiscal crisis has demonstrated the danger of chronic borrowing to cover local budget deficits.

Figure 5: INCREASE IN PRICES OF STATE AND LOCAL
GOVERNMENT PURCHASES, COMPARED WITH OTHER
ECONOMIC SECTORS, 1954–1974

Item	Price Increase (percent)[a]
State and local government purchases	152
Consumer goods and services	83
Private investment goods, total	91
Nonresidential structures	132

[a] GNP deflator for various sectors.

Source: *Economic Report of the President* (Washington, D.C.: U.S. Government Printing Office, February 1975).

The second response has usually been to cut government services or otherwise trim waste. Government officials and citizens have been forced to set priorities and eliminate marginally useful activities. Public-employee compensation, especially pensions, has become a target for attack. Cutting programs may be not only necessary but desirable in certain instances; it may well be that citizens' expectations of what government should provide have grown unrealistically or that some responsibilities assumed by government could be more satisfactorily met in other ways. In some instances, declines in the demand for public services have not been accompanied by commensurate reductions in staff. However, there is a limit to how drastically public services can be reduced without serious impact on the quality of life or without driving out citizens and businesses and thereby eroding the tax base. Moreover, cutbacks can work the greatest hardships on the politically weak and economically disadvantaged.

Only the third option, productivity improvement, offers a way of holding down costs without reducing the scope and quality of services.

For the present, reconciling the gap between revenues and expenditures may require a combination of all three options. But even if the revenue strain eases, state and local government productivity improvements, as we broadly define them to include quality and effectiveness as well as efficiency, offer one of the principal ways of improving overall economic well-being and the quality of life in the decades ahead.

EVIDENCE OF PRODUCTIVITY TRENDS

Without accepting the popular notion that most of what governments do is unproductive and hence wasteful, it is possible to list a number of factors inherent in public agencies that militate against productivity.

There are few political or administrative incentives to improve productivity. Top officials tend to aim for standards of performance that will keep public complaints at a tolerable level while keeping peace with civil servants.

Government has no force analogous to the profit motive to hold down costs. On the contrary, one criterion of success for some government administrators and their bureaucracies, which in most cases are monopolies, is their ability to obtain budget increases and to enlarge their staffs and their scope of activities. There are, to be sure, other forces that bear on government, including voter reaction, taxpayer resistance, consumer complaints, and credit ratings in capital markets. But none of these forces produces a specific measure that precisely and continuously links the cost of operations to the output of service agencies.

The politics of state and local governments have been oriented more toward the awarding of jobs, franchises, and contracts than toward delivery of services. This is one of the reasons why line-item budgets, which emphasize number of employees, materials, and equipment used, continue to be more popular than program budgets, which focus on the objectives of public services.

It is widely believed that some civil service and merit systems, originally intended as instruments to protect against political abuse, have tended to degenerate into instruments for protecting mediocrity and weakening administrative control. This tendency may be strengthened by the increasing power of public-employee unions.

In addition, inferences about productivity trends can be drawn from the limited statistical data available. For example, although the number

Figure 6: INCREASES IN AVERAGE ANNUAL EARNINGS OF
PUBLIC EMPLOYEES IN COMPARISON WITH OTHER
ECONOMIC SECTORS, 1953–1973 (per full-time employee)

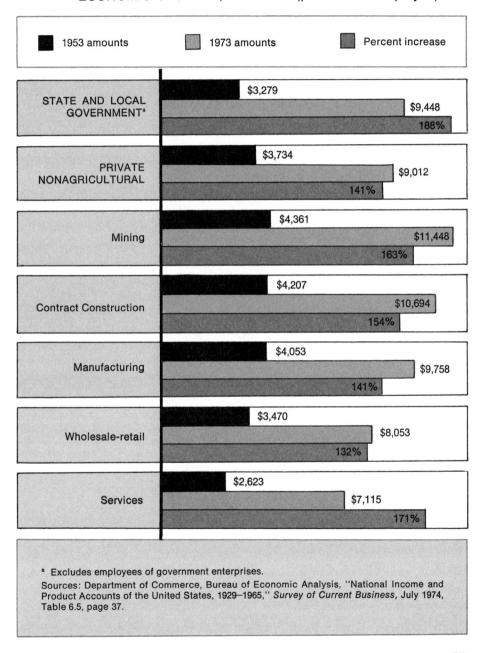

| 1953 amounts | 1973 amounts | Percent increase |

STATE AND LOCAL GOVERNMENT[a]
$3,279
$9,448
188%

PRIVATE NONAGRICULTURAL
$3,734
$9,012
141%

Mining
$4,361
$11,448
163%

Contract Construction
$4,207
$10,694
154%

Manufacturing
$4,053
$9,758
141%

Wholesale-retail
$3,470
$8,053
132%

Services
$2,623
$7,115
171%

[a] Excludes employees of government enterprises.
Sources: Department of Commerce, Bureau of Economic Analysis, "National Income and Product Accounts of the United States, 1929–1965," *Survey of Current Business,* July 1974, Table 6.5, page 37.

37

38

of state and local personnel increased by over 150 percent during the past two decades, there is no statistical evidence of commensurate increases in the quantity or quality of public services. A considerable amount of manpower has gone to make up for improvement of working conditions (decreased working hours, lighter workloads, and increased leave time). From 1953 to 1973, New York City's police force grew by 55 percent while the number of hours worked actually declined.[3]

Substantial differences in the costs and results of comparable services in different jurisdictions suggest disparities in productivity. Comparison of similar services furnished by private-sector agencies and public agencies usually reveals higher public-sector costs; where private-sector costs are higher, they are frequently set by businesses that are favored by government contracts. Similarly, expenditures per capita for different services vary greatly among cities; and after taking account of other reasons for differences, there remain strong implications of disparities in productivity.

Disparities occur not just because some poorly run jurisdictions register higher costs but also because others have achieved greater output and lower costs through the energy and imagination of public servants.

3/Inferences about state and local government productivity trends can also be drawn from the following type of analysis. The amount of inputs to state and local government production (measured by purchases of goods and services in constant dollars) rose by 182 percent from 1954 to 1974. The number of urban residents served increased by about 48 percent during the same period (urban residents are the best single proxy measurement for overall state and local government workload because most public services are concentrated in urban areas). The amount of inputs per resident thereby rose by 92 percent. The increase can be accounted for by one or more of four factors: increased workload (e.g., the number of public school pupils increased by about 58 percent; higher densities and changing compositions of population may also create greater needs for public services), broader scope of services (e.g., addition of recreation programs for the elderly), improved service quality (e.g., training police officers to handle family disputes more effectively), and decreased productivity.

Unless the first three factors accounted for a 92 percent increase (almost a doubling) of inputs per capita, productivity must have declined. This inference is partially supported by several studies that indicate declining productivity of individual services in selected cities. It may also be noted that the real input per capita of the federal government fell by 24 percent over the twenty-year period, suggesting a rise in federal productivity. This is consistent with the findings of the federal government's study of its own productivity.

Nevertheless, it should be stressed that it is not presently possible to measure overall state and local government productivity directly because it is impossible to assess with available data changes in the scope, quality, and workload of all state and local services or the extent to which some government services affect economic and social conditions.

Throughout the public sector, there are dedicated and effective employees who carry out their responsibilities with excellence. In fact, a principal impediment to productivity in state and local government is that capable people and agencies have not been recognized, supported, and freed of the constraints that prevent them from exercising leadership.

Deteriorating urban conditions suggest but do not necessarily signify lower productivity in specific government services. There is a limit, after all, to government's responsibility and capability for resolving problems. Productivity might increase and yet not correct every urban ill. For example, police services may become more effective, but if the conditions that produce crime (such as unemployment, poverty, and family turmoil) worsen, crime may continue to increase.*

Nevertheless, if public expenditures are increased to improve conditions and no improvement is perceived, we must ask whether the resources are being well used. Is there evidence, for example, that increased public expenditures have raised general health levels, affected recidivism among persons convicted of crime, checked the deterioration of large cities, or raised the quality of urban life in any substantial way? If not, are there alternative means of using those resources to achieve the conditions desired or for other purposes? Only when government efficiency and effectiveness have reached their highest possible levels and conditions are still not satisfactory can we conclude with assurance that government has reached the limits of its cost-effective contribution to improving the quality of life.**

But in the end, concern about productivity and the evidence of its current status depend largely upon what people expect and feel they are getting from government. Public opinion polls indicate that a large majority of the American people do not think they get their money's worth from the taxes they pay, yet most people believe that state and local government *can* be well run. It is this gap between what people expect from government and what they believe it is delivering that ultimately defines public perceptions of government productivity. We conclude, similarly, that state and local government productivity on the average is lower than it could be, but we are also convinced that the talents and energies of public managers and employees, a wealth of useful techniques and other resources, and especially, more effective political action to push for improved government can close that gap or help to redefine the dimensions of public expectations.

*See memorandum by CHARLES P. BOWEN, JR., page 84.
**See memorandum by JAMES Q. RIORDAN, page 84.

Opportunities
for Improving Productivity

IMPROVING GOVERNMENT PRODUCTIVITY ultimately requires greater incentive on the part of citizens, nongovernment groups, elected officials, professional managers, and public employees. In Chapter 4, we suggest approaches to increasing the overall motivation of government. In future policy statements, we intend to look in greater detail at the incentive structure of government.

However, the incentive to improve must be accompanied by, and interwoven with, the knowledge and ability to do so. There are four general areas of opportunity for improving state and local government productivity: management, the work force, technology and capital investment, and measurement.

STRENGTHENING MANAGEMENT

The most promising route to greater productivity is more effective management. Public-sector managers, including top elected executives, chief administrative officers, and department heads and supervisors, face conditions that are different from those confronting managers in the private sector, including community politics, civil service restrictions, and a work force that is also a major political constituency. Nevertheless, these public managers are responsible for establishing objectives, choosing programs, and assuring that policy is implemented effectively and efficiently. Their ability and, especially, their desire to do so are the keys to improvement.

The incentives for improved management have been weak in many jurisdictions. Elected officials generally have little understanding of administration and in any case tend to be more preoccupied with resolving political conflict and building support for the future. This lack of interest in administration among elected officials in turn affects the first ranks of professional managers, who tend to be cautious about attempted improvements that may have political repercussions for their elected superiors and hence for themselves. Thus, it is not surprising that motivation is also weak among managers at lower levels.

The first requirement for improved productivity, therefore, is increased incentives for managers to manage. This must start at the top, with the elected executive, but it will be dependent upon political forces in the community that push for improvement and hence make productivity a politically attractive concept for those seeking elective office. Incentives for professional managers can be increased by clearly linking the performance of their agencies to their own salaries, prospects for promotion, and reputations.

But although increased management incentives are essential, they are not sufficient. Even the many highly motivated managers in state and local government are limited in what they can accomplish by a management process and machinery that impede productivity in each of three principal phases: planning and budgeting, decision making, and implementation (principally line-agency operations).

Planning and Budgeting. Planning and budgeting are commonly assigned to separate staff agencies. But the two activities are closely related because the last step in the planning process is the allocation of resources, a major function of budgeting.

Planning. Efforts to improve productivity begin with planning that anticipates needs and identifies alternative courses of action for meeting them. In the United States, planning at the local level has long been identified with the physical aspects of urban development and with items that enter into capital budgets, such as buildings, highways and streets, water and sewer mains, schools, and hospitals. Over time, the increasing range of responsibilities given to state and local governments, particularly in the areas of social and economic development, created new sets of planning needs. A growing recognition of the interrelationships of government functions led to demands for more comprehensive planning that brings a wide variety of government programs into systems in order to ascertain how various activities complement or oppose each other.

In theory, the most important contribution of planners working with budget personnel is the analysis and evaluation that enables chief executives and legislators to deal more effectively with agency requests and political pressures for funds. In practice, things are somewhat different.

When planning was widely introduced at the local level a generation ago, it was heralded as a new branch of government to be divorced from politics and carried on by quasi-independent commissions of experts and impartial citizens. Many such commissions were created and continue today. But because they are unattached to legislatures or executives and, therefore, to the decision-making process, they lack political power and have little influence on decisions.

Most planning is done by professionals in particular functions; more than anyone else, they set the standards of adequacy for government services. Like most specialists, they tend to equate service improvements with larger budgets: more teachers for better education, more policemen for greater safety, and more doctors and hospitals for better health. Such conclusions are often incorrect, which suggests that functional planning assumptions need to be scrutinized closely by top managers and by the public. Over the last ten years, planners have begun to pay more attention to public preferences and to develop ways of soliciting them, and many professional fads and biases that contradict popular wisdom have run their course and been discarded. The opposite danger, however, is that programs may be initiated more to appease public demand for action than because of any expert belief that they will be effective.

Thus, there is a need both to link planning closely to operations and to establish a higher and more detached level of planning that can evaluate the biases of functional planners in assessing past policies and identifying future requirements. Both needs require appropriate participation by citizens and consumer groups, as well as the attention of elected officials and professional managers.

Budgeting. The budget process, where choices must be made about which functions and programs get which shares of revenues, is the most important focus of decision making at the highest levels. It is also a battleground for consumer groups who want more services, public employees who want more pay, administrators who want more resources for their programs, and increasingly, taxpayers who want to hold down taxes. The budget may increase programs to meet expanding needs and eliminate them when they outlive their usefulness; furthermore, it may reward efficient departmental performance and penalize ineffective performance.

However, budgets are seldom used as instruments for allocating resources by rules of benefit-to-cost or other analysis. They are subject to many pressures. For most governments, the overriding issues are wages, fringe benefits, pensions, and other employee compensation, rather than programs and agency functions. Conventional budgeting tends to use rules of thumb such as keeping agencies on a rough parity with respect to appropriation increases (if the police department gets an increase this year, the fire department will be in line for one next year). In some jurisdictions, automatic increases are mandated for all agencies; consequently, there is usually little surplus (unless it comes through a state or federal grant) for the initiation of any new program or for experimentation or innovation that could improve productivity.

Poor budget practices also inhibit fiscal planning. If it is easier to obtain funds by borrowing than from taxes, there will be a tendency to crowd the capital budget with everything possible, including expense items. New York City, which pioneered the concept of capital and expense budgets, engaged in this practice; as a consequence, its debt soared to the point where its securities could not be marketed.

Program-performance budgeting, which flowered briefly in the 1950s and again in the 1960s under the name of *planning-program-budgeting systems* (PPBS), emphasized the definition of missions and objectives. It also stressed analysis of the means to accomplish them, selection of the most cost-effective approaches, and evaluation of the results in terms of unit costs, effects on program clientele, conformity with objectives, and possibilities of improvement. PPBS has been largely discarded by the federal government and has been adopted by only a few state and local governments. Its lack of success has been attributed to several factors, including the difficulty of establishing clear measures of performance, inadequate staff to undertake the analysis required, overselling by zealous proponents, and the failure of top officials to support it because they are generally more interested in expenditure control than in cost-effective allocation of resources among programs.

Nevertheless, program-performance budgeting still provides one of the few administrative mechanisms for compelling a systematic consideration of priorities, program accomplishment, and the weighing of accomplishment against cost. Appendix A describes one example of how it encouraged a more careful consideration of the cost and impact of highway patrol in Pennsylvania by professional police administrators, elected legislators, and program analysts.

Program, performance, and line-item budgeting techniques can be combined to take advantage of the strengths of each. Related techniques include *zero-based budgeting*, which requires examination of existing programs as well as proposed additions, and *management by objective* (MBO), which attempts to compel examination of program purpose and its translation into specific and measurable targets. To be effective, such techniques must be backed up by accounting and reporting systems that can provide compatible cost and performance information.

Decision Making. Government policies and decisions tend to evolve through the planning and budgeting process, which sets the agenda for top decision makers. Yet, final policy decisions are usually taken without systematic analysis of various alternatives in terms of their likely costs and benefits.

Two categories of analysis can be distinguished, one having to do with policy or top-level decision making and the other with operations. Although the two overlap on many points, each involves different types of analytic expertise.

Policy analysts must weigh alternatives using facts that are frequently inadequate or hard to locate. However, data must be not only generated but also analyzed and presented to decision makers in a useful form.

The essence of decision analysis involves the technique of benefit-cost analysis; a ratio of benefits to costs of less than one raises a red flag for any course of action. Along with measurable benefits and costs, positive and negative effects that cannot readily be quantified must be taken into account, including environmental impact, political consequences, and administrative feasibility.

Analysis must also consider the degree of uncertainty involved in projecting the future because the value of projected benefits is diminished by uncertainty. One way of dealing with uncertainty is to calculate the probabilities of different outcomes. Another is simply to increase knowledge; lack of obtainable facts is an avoidable cause of uncertainty. Still another approach is to avoid commitments to large, expensive, and irreversible courses of action, thereby preserving flexibility in future decisions.

Educational preparation for policy analysis should include an appreciation of the values of systematic analysis and training in data sources, quantitative techniques (including the more commonly used mathematical

ACCOUNTING FOR UNCERTAINTY

A study of water-supply needs for northern New Jersey and southern New York exemplifies different means of accounting for uncertainty.

The study used as a criterion a maximum .01 probability that water supplies would fall as much as 20 percent below projected needs in any one year. This implies building a dam capacity for contingencies that on the average will not occur more often than once in a century. Water supplied by facilities that will be used only once in a century is very expensive. This suggests the search for other, less expensive alternatives such as standby and desalination plants, hauling water in from other areas, or simple conservation measures.

tools), and decision analysis, not to mention the nurturing of good judgment and common sense.

Some state and local governments have improved their analytic capability, but most are still seriously understaffed and otherwise ill-equipped. In some cases, they fail to recognize the potential contributions of the analytic approach or tend to regard analysts as overly theoretical and insufficiently aware of the complexities of decision making in a political setting (indeed, such criticism may often be justified). In other cases, legislatures, tending to be jealous of chief executives, attempt to restrict them by refusing to appropriate funds for staff assistance.

Many state legislatures and county and city councils require more adequate staff assistance in analyzing both budget requests and proposed legislation. Most legislative bodies currently enact laws with little formal analysis of costs and benefits or of the available alternatives. Committee hearings rarely fill this need because they tend to produce spotty or biased information. One approach is to require that all bills be accompanied by a report that indicates goals and objectives, justification of need, procedures and costs of implementation, experience with similar policies in other jurisdictions, criteria or measures by which accomplishment should be evaluated, and responsibility and procedures for evaluation.

By assessing plans and projects formulated by seldom-dispassionate departmental advocates, skillful analysis can overcome some of the pressures of the political milieu and even achieve political weight in its own right. Few political decision makers care to risk going against the facts, although there may be differences of opinion about the facts and what they imply.

Managing the Line Agencies. Most public agencies sincerely profess to serve the public, but the realities of the administrative process militate heavily against productivity. The principal influence is continual political pressure, which weighs in two directions. On the one hand, managers hesitate to undertake risky innovations for fear of laying themselves open to criticism in the future. On the other hand, political pressure frequently induces them to undertake courses of action that have small chance of succeeding and to maintain them even after they have demonstrably failed.

Public agencies tend to resist productivity-oriented innovations that require extra effort and disturb traditional work routines. Those who advocate change are often regarded with hostility or ignored.

RESISTANCE TO CHANGE

Inglewood, California, has used one-man refuse trucks for more than a decade at significantly reduced cost and with fewer injuries and greater satisfaction for personnel.

Informed of the one-man trucks, the sanitation director in an eastern city using four men to a truck said he did not believe it. Having confirmed that they were in use, he opined that Inglewood's streets and contours were different from his city's. Convinced that conditions in both places were generally the same, he lamented that his constituents would never accept the lower level of service. Persuaded that the levels of service were equal, he explained that the sanitation men would not accept a faster pace and harder work conditions. Told that the Inglewood sanitation men prefer the system because they set their own pace and suffer fewer injuries caused by careless co-workers, the director prophesied that the city council would never agree to such a large cutback in manpower. Informed of Inglewood's career development plan to move sanitation men into other city departments, the director pointed out he was responsible only for sanitation.

In theory, line agencies simply carry out functions and programs that are established by either constitutional and statutory provisions or decisions of policy makers; in practice, they play a large role in determining those policies and their administration. Protected by civil service tenure, middle-level administrators can in effect veto policy by controlling information and access and by simply not implementing or enforcing policies. By selectively magnifying the enforcement of certain policies, they can aggravate constituencies and cause political embarrassment for elected officials.

Civil service systems, conceived to minimize political interference, also limit the power of management to reward superior performance through promotion and salary increases and to penalize poor performance through pay cuts or discharges.

Many agencies consciously fight for independence from central controls. For example, the professional bureaucracies (such as police, education, and health) can muster successful public protest campaigns against "political interference" by top executives in matters pertaining to evaluation of needs, assignment and promotion of personnel, and operating routines.

Being insulated both from any pressure akin to the profit motive and from the need to be reelected, some public administrators become increasingly unresponsive to citizens' needs and impervious to review and change. Bureaucratic rules originally established to ensure regular and efficient operation tend to be used to protect personnel from evaluation according to more relevant standards of performance. The problem is exacerbated by an incentive structure that imposes heavy penalties for failure but little reward for superior performance.

Chronic deficiencies in line-agency management. A number of deficiencies arising from these administrative conditions directly impede productivity (although the degree to which they are manifested varies greatly, from jurisdictions with poor records to those that have achieved a high level of performance).

Weak agency management and lackadaisical supervision. Many top administrators are chosen for service or contributions to the party in power. Others are selected according to their professional qualifications; for example, health departments are commonly headed by medical doctors, police departments by policemen, engineering departments by engineers, and education departments by educators. Executives selected in either manner rarely have formal training in management and may have little or no management experience or ability.

Inefficient central controls. Because of the difficulty of imposing direct control from the top, chief executives confronted with the necessity of economizing tend to rely on such measures as niggling line-item budget controls, job freezes, and purchasing restrictions, rather than determining ways to improve performance.

Inefficient personnel methods. The ineffective organization of personnel, low work standards, and frequently, ingrained featherbedding combine to form inefficient and costly personnel practices.

Excessively detailed regulations and procedural routines. Many of these have been installed over the years to prevent repetition of politically costly scandals. Accordingly, even where such precautions notably deter productivity, they continue to be tolerated.

Ineffective communication within the agency and between line agencies and the chief executive. Jealousy over administrative prerogatives or sheer inertia inhibits communication, especially outside regular hierarchical channels.

Weak middle management. A common reason for weak middle management is closed systems of promotion based on examinations that frequently have little to do with administrative capacity or experience.

Lack of regard for convenience of clientele. This occurs in scheduling hours for health clinics and other service agencies that conflict with clients' working hours, delays in issuing permits, and failure to respond to complaints. Attempts to counter such tendencies include decentralization of services and other techniques that bring operating agencies closer to citizen-consumers.

Petty and not-so-petty graft. The most common form of graft involves the withholding of service or granting of special service by public servants pending illicit payment by the citizen-consumer. Another type involves collusion among public employees; for example, a supervisor permits a worker to build up overtime shortly before he retires in order to increase the size of his pension.

Lack of awareness or failure to adopt technologies that have been successful. A few agencies have developed a tradition of technological innovation, but most display little interest in new techniques.

There are no shortcuts to correcting such deficiencies. The principal requirement is the will of top managers to use the knowledge and the many resources and techniques already available to improve administration. In some instances, however, specialized assistance may be required.

EXAMPLES OF IMPROVING EFFICIENCY

Opportunities for improving efficiency in line-agency operations are almost infinite.

The system of deploying snow plows in a large city has been improved by a strategy that classified highways and streets so that they could be cleared in the order of their importance to the restoration of traffic flow, assigned vehicles to routes according to the established priorities, and parked vehicles at specified deployment points whenever snowfalls were forecast.

Costs of maintaining a municipally owned automobile fleet were analyzed and found to be 30 to 50 percent higher than the cost of leasing equivalent vehicles. This finding led to an experimental leasing program and measures designed to raise productivity in the city's maintenance shops, which were found to be responsible for part of the high costs.

A program of alerting police officers in advance of changes in scheduled court appearances helped to eliminate unnecessary appearances for arresting officers. (This program reported a potential annual savings in the time of arresting officers of 200 man years.)

A study of the lifetime costs of sanitation and fire trucks resulted in a policy of shorter-term replacement to reduce maintenance costs and the amount of time vehicles were out of service.

Analysis in line agencies. In addition to the need for policy analysis, there is a need for analysis of management and programs in operation in two principal areas.

Effectiveness of organization and communications. This concerns the relationship between the functions performed by the agency and its organizational structure, the balance between responsibility and delegation of authority, the flow of intra-agency communication, the quality of supervision at various levels, internal personnel relations and morale, and related organizational questions. Analysis in these areas requires skills from a range of disciplines, including business and public administration and the behavioral sciences.

USE OF ANALYTIC TOOLS

The application of more sophisticated analytic tools makes it possible to optimize particular objectives in certain types of decisions.

For example, linear programming techniques can determine where to place fire stations in order to minimize the average time required to respond to alarms in an area with a given number of fire stations. Alternatively, given the average response time desired, the number of fire stations required can be specified. Similarly, programming can determine the most efficient garbage collection routes, optimum deployment of police cars, and other means to deploy resources more efficiently.

Management engineering. This includes tools for improving the technical efficiency of production processes and techniques for reducing costs. Such analysis requires industrial engineering skills, supplemented by other technical specialties, such as cost accounting and statistics.

Management engineering typically focuses on a number of factors: detailed definition of objectives and tasks to be performed, identification of resources needed (people with particular skills, equipment, facilities, and so forth), design of organization procedure, allocation of resources by time and place (deployment of personnel to match work force to workload, scheduling of activities to minimize time requirements and assure smooth work flow, assignment of tasks to match responsibilities to personnel abilities and to assure even distribution of work, inventory control for timely delivery and efficient use of materials), mechanisms for control and monitoring of activity, and evaluation of accomplishment.[1]

In addition to possessing the necessary technical skills, it is essential that the effective analyst understand the political and administrative milieu in which government agencies function and consider the strategy and process by which the inevitable roadblocks to change can be overcome and improvements actually implemented. It is important to remember that

1/See Appendix B, "Examples of Improvement in Line-Agency Operations."

mathematical modeling cannot fully account for the complexity of social and political phenomena and that analysis undertaken without attention to the practical problems of implementation will be wasted or, worse, counterproductive.

Developing Management Personnel. In addition to more effective incentives and techniques, strengthening management depends upon the quality of managers themselves. There is no apparent dearth of potential managers available to state and local agencies; lack of capable managers and analytic staff on the job lies rather in the failure of agencies to find and develop them. Steps that can be taken include paying competitive salaries to attract top managers from business, other governments, and the nonprofit sector; improving training in administration for managers from professional fields such as engineering, health, and police; giving more weight to managerial potential in promotion from the ranks (the principal source of most government managers) and more training for those newly recruited into supervisory positions; and developing entry-level management training, analytic, and staff positions and career paths to take advantage of the increasing number of graduates from university programs in public management.

WORK FORCE

Although government operations are labor-intensive, the prospects for substantial replacement of manpower with capital equipment do not appear to be as great as they have been in other economic activities, such as agriculture. Consequently, productivity gains in government will depend heavily on better use of the talents and energies of its employees, which is principally a management responsibility.

The predominant force affecting the disposition of workers in government is the growth of public-employee unions. The political influence of government workers has increased as their numbers have grown in proportion to the voting population and as they have become better organized. Public employees are also exercising increasing influence directly on the management of government through collective bargaining.

Public-sector collective bargaining is still in the formative stages. The procedures and traditions that are established now will determine whether future labor-management relations enhance productivity or impede it to the detriment of both employees and the public. Timely action is all the more important because unions are still growing, principally by enlisting employees already on the payroll; in later years, they may seek to increase personnel requirements or more strenuously resist reductions in force that would shrink their membership. Elected officials and top managers need to acquire and exercise both the understanding and the professional expertise in labor relations necessary to protect the interests of both the public and the employees. Several public-interest groups have recognized this need by establishing the Labor-Management Relations Service (based in Washington, D.C.) to provide local government officials across the country with information and education on the rapid developments occurring in public-sector labor relations.

For better or worse, collective bargaining may erode or supplant parts of traditional civil service systems. Meanwhile, however, civil service systems need to be scrutinized for evidence of counterproductive tendencies. There is evidence that some systems, in an effort to formalize the presumed principle of merit and minimize political influence, have instead reinforced mediocrity and otherwise impeded productivity.

In addition, there is the question of how the talents and energies of workers can be more productively applied to ongoing activities so that both the employee and the public will benefit. One simple approach is more extensive use of conventional incentive techniques (such as work standards and bonus payments) that have long been used in business. Such techniques may be of limited utility, however, in those functions where management has little direct control over service delivery at the crucial point of contact between government and citizens. In many activities, the critical individual is the one who delivers services or otherwise represents government directly: the policeman, the teacher, the physician or nurse, the caseworker. No policy directives or management controls can incorporate the subtlety and detail needed to guide a policeman in dealing with ambiguous or delicate situations or a teacher trying to respond to differing student needs and problems.

Experiments in the private sector suggest that such approaches as the redesign of jobs and increased employee participation in the management process may, to a clearly limited extent, improve productivity while increasing employee satisfaction. It is uncertain how applicable these experiments are to government. But it is clear that the organization and management of public services should recognize and account for the high degree of responsibility and independence of workers in key functions.

The Committee intends to address these and related issues in a subsequent policy statement.

TECHNOLOGY AND CAPITAL INVESTMENT

Two major factors in raising the productivity of the private sector have been technological advances (not just in hardware but in improved knowledge and methods as well) and increases in the ratio of capital to labor (more equipment per worker).

Technology has had less impact in the public sector. Most government agencies are reluctant to experiment with new techniques and procedures. In many cases, experimentation with new methods and tools or with new types of equipment has failed or has far exceeded projected costs.

Because the state and local government market is poorly understood and the requirements of government agencies vary in size and other characteristics, private firms devote relatively little time and money to research and development of new products for the public sector.

A notable exception has been the attention given to computers, which have had several advantages. Because they are standard products with a wide variety of applications in both the public and the private sectors, computers could be immediately adapted to government operations. They are also aggressively marketed. Nevertheless, many jurisdictions still lag behind in even the more common uses of computers, especially data handling, which constitutes a large proportion of routine government operations. Governments that are too small to operate a computer economically could explore the use of time-sharing arrangements with other governments or computer firms. Numerous opportunities remain for improving efficiency through computer operations, for example, in health services and welfare administration.

However, most public technology suffers from the lack of such advantages and requires more conscious development by public officials themselves. Greater effort is required for identifying and communicating their needs to potential suppliers of technologies, creating greater awareness of new technologies already available, and providing the funds and staff for investigating, adapting, and installing new machinery and equipment.

In order to help overcome such obstacles, the International City Management Association and other public-interest groups sponsored, with federal assistance, the creation of Public Technology, Inc. PTI was charged with stimulating the development of new technology for the public sector, disseminating information about its findings, and encouraging the adoption of technology. Its initial emphasis on hard technology has expanded to include soft technology or systems engineering, reflecting both the difficulty of hardware application to government services and the increasing stress on responding to needs identified by local administrators.

Interest in the more dramatic examples of technological application should not divert administrators from developing the potential for better management of the maintenance and replacement of standard equipment and of the design and construction of new facilities. Government agencies use a wide range of technology, including standard office equipment,

---

TECHNOLOGICAL APPLICATIONS IN THE PUBLIC SECTOR

Rapid Water. The well-known case of rapid water for fire fighting illustrates the difficulties of getting acceptance for new processes from government bureaucracies and of inducing industry to respond to a demonstrated need. New York City Rand Institute technicians suggested to the city's fire department that the addition of a polymer, which had been discovered sometime previously but never utilized for this purpose, could reduce the friction of water flowing through a fire hose and thereby increase the volume of water delivered by as much as 50 to 70 percent. A substantial effort was required to interest fire officials, but the more surprising problem was the reluctance of several firms approached to undertake the development. After the product was available, it took the fire department several years to begin equipping its pumpers with equipment to utilize the technology.

School Building Design. A joint venture by several California school districts, funded by Educational Facilities Laboratories, Inc., to improve school construction resulted in a better, lower-cost product that has been widely emulated in the United States.

The group first put together a large market by enlisting a score of schools planning to build new facilities. Performance specifications for building components, based on careful surveys, were prepared for heating, ventilation, and cooling systems; ceiling-lighting systems; and division of interior space. Bids were invited from manufacturers of products that would meet these specifications, with the aggregated market being the prize for winners.

---

automotive vehicles, and costly construction equipment. The federal government's study of its own productivity determined that many government administrators, more accustomed to dealing with labor-intensive than with technology-intensive operations, miss opportunities for cost savings and productivity improvements through more skillful investment and management of capital equipment and planning for the construction of major facilities. Too often, new facilities are planned without taking into consideration the costs involved in operating them or the potential for minimizing operating and maintenance costs through better design. Such opportunities are abundantly available in states and localities.

MEASURING GOVERNMENT ACTIVITIES

The purpose of quantitative measurement is to increase precision in assessing effectiveness and efficiency. Too often, however, attempts to tack numbers onto activities that do not lend themselves to quantification create confusion and misunderstanding. Moreover, there is always the risk that data will be distorted. For example, refuse can be watered down to increase tonnage; crime figures can be doctored upward to demonstrate the need for higher budgets or downward to show improved performance; low base rates can be established to magnify future improvements. Taken together, however, a series of appropriate measures can aid professional judgment and public understanding of how performance compares with an established standard of achievement, with past performance levels of the same agency, and with performance levels of other jurisdictions and private agencies.

Some services can be easily quantified, such as tons of refuse collected and miles of streets swept. However, many public services cannot be neatly packaged and quantitatively measured in all aspects. Police services exemplify such measurement difficulties. Crime rates are an unsatisfactory index of police effectiveness in deterring crime because the propensity toward crime also depends upon age levels, economic circumstances, and other demographic factors over which police departments have no control. The number of so-called quality arrests (those that result in indictments or convictions) is more meaningful than the total number of arrests but still provides only a partial measure of effectiveness. The number of miles patrolled is primarily a measure of workload and may or may not contribute to effectiveness.

Similarly, productivity in education is difficult to measure both because many of the goals of education are intangible and because complex outside factors come into play. A decline in reading scores does not necessarily indicate a drop in the productivity of public schools; it might also reflect a change in the composition of the school population. However, a sustained rise in reading scores does not necessarily indicate better teaching; it might result from increased enrollment of students from family backgrounds that stimulate learning.

Three types of measures can assist managers in improving productivity.

General Social Conditions. Unemployment, income levels, health standards, environmental conditions, and other social indicators are useful guides in general planning and evaluation, even though they do not necessarily reflect the consequences of government action exclusively. Interest in social indicators has grown partly as an alternative or a supplement to the heavy reliance on measures of purely economic well-being (especially GNP), which do not adequately account for other public goals or activities relating to the quality of life.

Program Effectiveness. Measures can help to assess the direct and intermediate results of agency programs; for example, the performance of pupils on standardized tests and the condition of streets (as indicated by the absence of potholes). In some cases, such indicators come as close as one can get to measuring actual success in meeting ultimate objectives; for example, the number of licenses issued is one ultimate and easily measurable objective of a motor vehicle department. In other cases, they are only surrogate indicators of progress toward ultimate objectives; for example, teacher-pupil ratios are not indicators of overall education productivity; they reflect a workload that is presumed to have some bearing on teaching effectiveness.

Survey or polling techniques can provide managers with useful information for assessing citizen satisfaction with services, determining the profile of service users, uncovering complaints that ordinarily would not emerge, and identifying future service needs. For example, the orientation of one city recreation program was changed from team sports to individual craft activities on the basis of a user-preference survey. Police administrators have used so-called victimization surveys of the general population to gather more accurate information than is provided by conventional crime reports on crime incidence, public feelings of security, and confidence in the police force.

Program Efficiency. Numerous quantitative indicators can provide partial information on agency activity or workload; examples include numbers of lines typed, inspections completed, cases handled, and applications processed. Such measures, when calculated on an hourly or dollar basis and controlled for quality, can provide information that is useful to managers in assessing agency efficiency. Typical efficiency measures include physical units of output per unit of labor (tons of refuse collected per manhour), physical units of output per dollar of expenditure (tons of refuse collected per dollar expended on refuse collection), throughput time (hours required to process a request for a plumbing license), downtime (percent of time that police cars are out of operation because of repairs), and capacity utilization (percent of total potential computer time actually used).

Data can also be used to compare dollar expenditures or personnel employed on a per capita or per user basis for similar functions in different jurisdictions (such as policemen per 100,000 population or dollars spent per student). Although large differences in these figures may result from factors other than productivity (such as differences in employee compensation, levels of service provided, or environmental conditions), they raise meaningful questions for further analysis.

To be useful, information on government performance must be readily available and closely linked to decision makers through usable information systems (which often can be computerized) and the budget process. (See Appendix C, "Management Information System Development and Application.")

Strengthening Forces
That Can Motivate Government
Productivity

FAILURE TO EXPLOIT the many opportunities for improving productivity is not so much the fault of any public official or worker as it is the result of a political and administrative incentive structure that militates against effective and efficient performance. The responsibility for altering this structure to increase motivation for productivity depends largely on more effective pressure from the citizens who elect public officials, pay taxes, and consume public services. However, voter reaction combines with, and is influenced by, other forces and mechanisms that can induce better administration of public programs. These forces include formal mechanisms for evaluating performance and holding officials accountable, competition from other public and private agencies that aspire to perform the same service, and productivity impetus from outside groups that can muster political pressure or supply expertise.

FORMAL MECHANISMS FOR EVALUATING SERVICES

The first line of defense against government inefficiency and misfeasance is the power to investigate and expose. Such powers are vested in legislative bodies and in officials formally responsible to legislatures or elected directly by the public.

Auditing Agencies. One traditional check on the performance of government agencies is the external audit. Most state governments and many of the larger municipalities have independently elected comptrollers or auditors responsible for protecting the public against abuses by elected officials or other administrators. State governments also have the power to impose accounting and budgeting requirements on their municipalities and to perform audits of municipal accounts (or require audits by private certified public accountants). However, there are several important deficiencies in the audit function as it is ordinarily practiced.

Historically, auditors have concentrated on public financial accounts and on the legality and propriety of public expenditures rather than on program effectiveness and the functional efficiency of government programs. But even so, they frequently fail to check even the more common forms of political finagling, such as manipulating contracts toward favored bidders. Many such officers spend major effort on the administrative function of preaudit (certifying vouchers for payment) instead of evaluating the activities and performance for which expenditures are made.

Many auditing officers are responsible only to the general public, which has no means of holding them accountable except the power to vote them out of office. Some elected auditors exploit their offices for political purposes, and although this tendency is inevitable in a political system, it can be carried to lengths that damage the credibility of the audit function. The states generally make only cursory audits of municipalities, and these are frequently years late.

These deficiencies suggest various kinds of administrative reforms, most of which have ample precedent at the federal or state and local levels.

Over the years, the U.S. General Accounting Office (the auditor for the federal government) has concentrated increasingly on the effectiveness of government operations and the accomplishment of objectives. GAO emphasizes three elements of government audit: financial and compliance requirements, economy and efficiency, and program results (commonly referred to as *performance auditing*).[1]

At the state and local government level, effective performance auditing would require better standards and evaluative criteria than now exist.

1/Comptroller General of the United States, *Standards for Audit of Governmental Organizations, Programs, Activities and Functions* (Washington, D.C.: U.S. General Accounting Office, 1972).

An even more serious impediment is the lack of personnel with the skills required for a competent and impartial performance evaluation. GAO, in cooperation with the International City Management Association, undertook a pilot effort to apply the concept of performance auditing in thirteen local governments. They have identified some ways in which the performance audit process needs to be modified to make it responsive to the needs of local governments.

Public auditors should be responsible to an agency, ordinarily the legislature, with power to bring pressure for improvement. The comptroller general of the United States and GAO, for example, are responsible primarily to Congress, and many of their investigations are undertaken upon specific congressional requests.

In principle, the auditing officer should be responsible to the legislature (as is the case in some states), but his reports as a rule should be made public; he should not be muzzled by a legislative majority. What is needed is a balance of forces that, on the one hand, will restrain the auditing officer from speaking irresponsibly and using his office to build a political base and, on the other hand, will ensure an effective and professional assessment of the performance by the executive branch.

However, the function of the auditing officer is limited. For example, it is not broad enough to protect citizens from incursions on their rights or from abuse or undue deprivation by public agencies or to deal with the day-to-day impact of agency operations on neighborhoods and individuals.

Performance Evaluation with Political Impact. A principal weakness in state and local political systems is the absence of any institution that can impartially assess government performance free from the direct pressures of partisan politics yet with the necessary public visibility and prestige to create incentives for improvement. An expanded audit function may be a partial remedy, but as long as auditing is a part of government, it must maintain a strict professionalism that limits its ability to build on public support to advocate change. Otherwise, it risks becoming a political vehicle for elected officials, who are hardly disinterested in public perceptions of government performance. Private good-government groups, on the other hand, generally lack sufficient and independent financing that frees professional staff from the need to cater to the special-interest groups that sponsor them.

What is needed are independent institutions that can command both public attention and public respect and that have assured sources of funds and professional capability to assess government performance regularly, systematically, and publicly. Such qualities are, of course, difficult to combine in a single institution. One possibility is joint funding by government and private organizations. Another would be the creation by state or federal law of a quasi-public corporation either to undertake such work or to provide public funds to organizations that can.

The purpose of such an institution would be the continuous evaluation of government performance, employing analytic techniques of measurement and evaluation, as a means of giving recognition to superior performance and of exposing inadequate performance. One of its activities, for example, would be to publicize the absence of performance data in such functions as police, health, and sanitation departments and to demonstrate the potential for improvement by actually developing and analyzing performance data. Another activity would be to develop and publicize comparative data on the cost and accomplishment of similar functions in different jurisdictions.

PROMOTING COMPETITION
AND CONSUMER CHOICE

The monopolistic character of most public-service agencies is often cited as a main reason for their lack of interest in productivity. The inefficiency of municipal services cannot be entirely accounted for by ineffective mayors, managers, workers, unions, or labor leaders; it is in large measure a natural consequence of a monopoly system.

Even where similar services can be purchased from private organizations, the tax-supported public agency still has the advantage of providing its services without direct charge. For example, even when parents enroll their children in private schools because of relative dissatisfaction with public schools, they continue to finance public education through taxes, and the public system does not suffer a loss of revenue along with the loss of pupils.

Traditional public administration theory correctly points to overlapping or duplicate functions as possible sources of inefficiency; however, for some activities, the competition that arises from providing a choice of services may produce productivity gains that more than compensate for the possible diseconomies of operating two or more organizations that provide similar services.

Service Competition.   Competition can be enhanced in several ways. Private suppliers can be allowed to compete with government agencies on reasonably equal terms. This alternative may be applied to certain government enterprises, a notable example being the Postal Service. In many cases, private carriers undertake functions similar to those performed by the U.S. Postal Service with greater productivity for reasons traceable to clear differences in management and operating procedures.

Another technique that has been tested, with mixed results, is to provide clients with vouchers or other forms of purchasing power so that they may choose among suppliers, which may be public or private agencies (e.g., rent supplements that allow low-income families to rent from private landlords, as an alternative to public housing).

Still another means of extending consumer choice and realizing benefits of competition may be intragovernmental competition. Government agencies frequently compete among themselves, and in some circumstances, such competition may be desirable. For example, a school district may offer a choice among elementary schools rather than requiring pupils to attend a particular school. Alternatives to public services can also be offered by the large nonprofit sector, which can meet the desires of special constituencies in recreation, health, education, research, and other areas. However, nonprofit organizations should apply the same practices for improving productivity that we are suggesting for government.

Contracting Services.   Government agencies may contract for the performance of tax-financed services (which otherwise would be performed in-house) with either public agencies or private organizations.

Contracting with private firms has been most successful in those operations that have clearly measurable outputs, such as refuse collection, construction, food service operations, transportation services, street cleaning and repair, snow removal, and maintenance services. Some jurisdictions, for example, have discovered that the food service operations in educational institutions, transportation for public schools, and even maintenance for public buildings may be more cheaply and in some cases more effectively provided by private companies that specialize in service operations.

There are several possible advantages to choosing this option. Contracts with large producers may enable economies of scale to be realized by spreading production over a larger number of units than the contracting jurisdiction requires. Contracting may also enable governments to avoid legally imposed restrictive controls (budgetary, personnel, and other) that reduce administrative flexibility. Economies may also be realized where private-sector salaries and/or fringe benefits are lower than those of government workers.

Contracting governments can also benefit from the competition among would-be suppliers and from the incentive of the profit motive to improve service efficiency and quality. In some instances, contracting with several smaller businesses for the same service may enhance competition and take advantage of the more efficient operations of contractors not burdened by high administrative overhead. One possibility, for example, may be to contract with two or more refuse collectors to service different sectors of the same jurisdiction.

Moreover, the process of switching from one service organization to another may improve performance by permitting old functions and outmoded procedures to be dropped or updated and by compelling a reexamination of purpose and strategy. The knowledge that another organization could perform the service may also provide incentives to the current service organization.

However, contracting also has its disadvantages. First, there is the problem of evaluation and quality control. Government agencies must themselves undertake to control the quality of services whether they are produced by government or nongovernment agencies. If the quantity or quality of the product is not easily measurable, control necessitates product inspections, investigations of complaints, and monitoring of production processes. Most government agencies are required by law to award contracts to the lowest bidder, even if the low-bidding firm is perceived as less effective than other firms. One answer to this problem is highly detailed contract specifications that establish both efficiency and quality standards, although care must be taken that such specifications do not create rigidities that impede efficient operation.

A second major problem concerns manipulation and graft. Government contracts are still a primary source of political patronage, and firms that seek government contracts have been a principal source of political financing. Revelations of corruption in government contracting have generated a public suspicion that at least matches public distrust of government bureaucracies. Governments that are inefficient or corrupt in providing public services will almost invariably manifest the same tendencies in administering contracts.

However, when all factors are taken into consideration, it is clear that contracting and competition among agencies, if judiciously used, can be a potent force in expanding the scope and content of government services and in checking potential abuses of government bureaucracies.

SUPPORT FOR PRODUCTIVITY
FROM OUTSIDE GROUPS

Ultimately, greater productivity in government will depend on the effectiveness of political pressure from voters, taxpayers, and consumers of government services. A number of groups in the political system can bring pressure to bear on government or otherwise offer support and expertise that can improve productivity.

Public-Interest and Government-Reform Groups. A number of research and reform groups over the years have compiled an impressive record of inducing improvement in government operations.

Local private research institutions. New York's Bureau of Municipal Research, for example, developed much of the apparatus of modern municipal government and stimulated the creation of numerous bureaus in other cities.

Taxpayers' associations. The Pennsylvania Economy League has been notable for the number and depth of its studies of policy issues and operations of Pennsylvania state and local governments.

National research and advocacy groups. The National Municipal League has promoted and been largely responsible for the success of the city-manager movement (40 percent of all American municipalities now use the professional manager form of government); developed model charters for county and municipal governments and model constitutions for state governments; served as a clearinghouse for information on developments in municipal planning, finance, and administration; and sponsored research on municipal policy issues.

League of Women Voters. This organization has provided effective analysis of issues and pushed for reforms at the national, state, and local levels.

In addition, emerging forces include a variety of citizen organizations that focus on local issues, nationally oriented groups such as John Gardner's Common Cause and Ralph Nader's Public Citizen that focus on improving government processes (both groups have more recently supported establishment of associated organizations at the state and local levels), and new nonprofit organizations that emphasize research and assistance to governments. An example in the latter category is the Fund for the City of New

York, established in 1968 by the Ford Foundation. The fund has chosen in recent years to concentrate on such projects as the development and utilization of performance measures in sanitation and municipal hospitals.

Different groups employ different strategies. One approach is an adversary strategy that analyzes and criticizes government policies and operations on the basis of data and observations assembled from the outside. Even at this level, opportunities for useful work are numerous.

Other groups attempt to cooperate with and assist government agencies, working from the inside and providing technical expertise. Here, success requires sources of expertise and receptivity on the part of the management and staff of the agency involved.

Business Groups. There are few public issues of greater importance to the local business community than improving the productivity of government. Traditionally, the business community has been a strong political force in states and localities across the country. In recent years, however, its influence has declined as emerging groups such as consumers, women, minorities, and neighborhood and civic associations have developed strength. We believe that businessmen should assert their leadership in the improvement of their communities. They need to reassess their own roles in relation to changed political conditions and to propose creative solutions to which they can lend both their influence and their expertise.

Many state and local chambers of commerce and other business groups such as the Economic Development Council of New York City have pushed for government reform and provided expertise to assist in administrative improvement. In North Carolina, the Governor's Efficiency Study Commission contributed 34,000 hours of private-sector executive time that identified a potential annual savings of $67 million and recommended numerous other measures for improving operations, 85 percent of which could be implemented directly by executive order.

In general, direct technical assistance supplied gratis by business is likely to be most useful in limited special situations that are akin to business operations. Business firms as a class can be most effective in improving the quality of state and local government by supporting professionally staffed research organizations and by active involvement and participation in state and local affairs.

Other Outside Groups. There are many other groups that can support actions to increase state and local government productivity. Organized labor, both public and private, is in a particularly advantageous position to press for productivity measures that can reduce costs without impairing service. Public employees are a prime source of information on productivity improvement; when combined with the research capabilities and organizational understanding of their unions, such knowledge could be an invaluable contribution to productivity improvement.

The mass media are the source of most public information about government operations. Informed interpretive reporting is essential to stimulating greater awareness not only of the deficiencies but also of the significant accomplishments of state and local government.

Political parties have much to gain by demonstrating genuine concern for providing government that is not only honest but efficient and capable of delivering on promises.

Universities and research centers can contribute much to public policy and productivity analysis. University departments of economics, business and public administration, industrial engineering, and psychology can provide training and research in planning, finance, and management. In the long run, the universities are the most important source of technical skills and trained professionals for improving the quality of government administration. At the secondary school level, social studies curricula should be redesigned and updated to provide a more realistic understanding of how state and local governments operate and to stress the importance of improving productivity in government.

Responsibilities in the Federal System for Improving State and Local Government Productivity

THE PRINCIPAL RESPONSIBILITY for improving state and local government productivity rests with the states and localities themselves and with the citizens they serve.* No standardized prescriptions could cover the varied economies, populations, and forms of government of America's 50 states and 39,000 municipalities, counties, and townships. Nor will any approaches prove successful without the enthusiastic and sustained backing of top state and local government officials and the cooperative support of public employees and citizens. State and local governments should act to improve their productivity through opportunities suggested in this policy statement for more effective identification of goals and objectives, choice of most cost-effective policies for achieving goals, and utilization of a range of techniques and practices to improve operations.

However, no state or local government functions independently; each interacts with other governments in the federal system in ways that impede or enhance productivity.*

*See memoranda by OSCAR A. LUNDIN, page 80.

STATE ROLE IN ENCOURAGING
LOCAL GOVERNMENT PRODUCTIVITY

The Constitution recognizes states as sovereign powers within the federal system and establishes, through a series of judicial rulings, their authority to create, abolish, and regulate local governments. The structural, financial, and administrative foundations established by state law directly affect the productivity of local governments, for better or worse. Thus, the issue is not whether states have a responsibility but rather how they should exercise their responsibility in order to enhance local government productivity.

We believe the state governments should play a central role in providing leadership, incentives, and technical assistance for improving the productivity of their local governments and, further, should work toward removing state-imposed impediments to productivity, which in many states are numerous. This does not imply a diminution of local prerogatives; on the contrary, it suggests a need for states to update their traditional responsibility for providing foundations of local government that will permit cities and counties to manage their own affairs more effectively.

To date, the states have had a mixed record of achievement. Outstanding examples of progress include Minnesota's creation of the Metropolitan Council of the Twin Cities Area, Indiana's consolidation of Marion County and Indianapolis into "Unigov," and Massachusetts's establishment of numerous regional authorities for its metropolitan areas. Consolidation of school districts has been carried out in nearly all states, partly in response to prodding by the federal government.

Most states, however, have done little to improve local government structure and even less to encourage more effective management. For example, although most states have accounting standards and uniform budgeting and accounting procedures, these are resisted by local governments and rarely enforced because of a lack of will on the part of state government.

In some instances, states not only fail to encourage productivity but may actually impede it. Legislatures, for example, have been vulnerable to demands of local government employee organizations in mandating staffing patterns, work rules, pension systems, and pay scales that obstruct management and increase costs. Thus, state legislation, until modified, prevented New York City from assigning more police to duty in high-crime periods. Failure to modernize state constitutions and statutes (in some instances the fault of citizens and local officials rather than of state leaders) results in local governments operating with structures and processes created for conditions prevailing in the nineteenth century.

Some state governments lag behind the more progressive local governments within their jurisdiction in matters of internal management. These localities will naturally resist impositions from a state that is considered inferior in management capability.

A long-overdue first step is for state government to provide the basic structural foundations for effective local government. Local government in the United States continues to be characterized by unnecessary duplicative and overlapping jurisdictions. There is a need for local jurisdictions of sufficient size and authority to plan, administer, and provide financial support for solutions to areawide problems. Yet, the same system should also provide for smaller units to permit the exercise of local power over matters directly affecting the community. The emphasis should be on the sharing of power between the metropolitan and community levels and not necessarily on the assignment of an entire function to either level.[1] **We recommend that state governments move vigorously to improve the structure of local government. Such measures should include the creation of regional, metropolitan, local, and neighborhood institutions; the redefinition or redistribution of government powers and functions; and the authorization to permit local units to utilize intergovernmental contracting and other cooperative service arrangements.***

Many local governments and operating agencies continue to be administered by persons who lack management training, experience, or capability. Even jurisdictions with city managers lack the management or other personnel required for the systematic improvement of policy making and operations. **We recommend that state governments encourage and assist smaller governments in enlisting professional management (such as the circuit city manager or other manpower-pooling arrangements) and larger units in providing management training for top administrators and creating full-time administrative units staffed by personnel professionally trained in management and analysis.**

The development and use of skilled professionals is also limited by restrictive personnel systems that discourage employees from moving to

---

1/See *Modernizing Local Government* (1966), *Modernizing State Government* (1967), and *Reshaping Government in Metropolitan Areas* (1970).

*See memorandum by FRAZAR B. WILDE, page 81.

new positions that can best use their capabilities as they gain experience and skills. We believe that pension portability should be established nationwide to permit greater mobility of public-sector personnel. Similar actions can also be initiated at the state level; this is especially important because states have legal authority over local government personnel systems. **We recommend that state and local government personnel systems be modified to allow employees to move among local and state agencies without loss of rank, seniority, or pension rights.*** Implementation of this recommendation will require creation of appropriate state mechanisms to determine the accounting and actuarial principles and other technical arrangements by which pension funds can be transferred from one system to another with appropriate adjustments to account for variations in pension formulas.

Although most states now require some form of fiscal audit of local governments, few have the legal provision or the administrative capacity for evaluating performance or even for the collection of comparative data on program costs and results. We believe that states must take a first step in this direction. **We recommend that state governments establish and enforce minimum standards for local government budgeting, accounting, and performance and reporting systems that would provide data on the level, quality, results, and costs of services.*** Such data would also provide the means for local governments themselves and for other government agencies, individual citizens, and public-interest groups to evaluate performance. Establishment of minimum (rather than uniform) standards would provide comparable data without impeding those local governments that have more advanced systems. Where enforcement proves difficult, states could require compliance as a condition for receiving state grants.

However, improved performance information will have little consequence without effective mechanisms to evaluate performance and take necessary steps toward improvement (as discussed in Chapter 4). **We recommend that the governor of each state establish a high-level commission with state, local, and nongovernment representation to identify and suggest permanent mechanisms for evaluating and improving state and local government productivity.** Such commissions should consider a range of options, including: expansion of the traditional audit function to include performance reporting and evaluation, assignment of the responsibility for periodically evaluating and assisting local government productivity efforts to a central state agency or a new unit in the office of the governor, establishment of a statewide system of comprehensive measurement of local government performance, and creation of a nongovernment or quasi-public institution with high visibility and professional staffing for the evaluation of state and local governments.

State governments should also provide financial and technical assistance to local governments for the purposes of developing and implementing performance measures, experimenting with or implementing techniques or programs that have the greatest likelihood of success, and undertaking other programs that would improve productivity. Few local governments have either the manpower or the funds to undertake such efforts; skillful application by states in key localities could effectively exert leverage on other cities and counties in the state.

In turn, certain local and substate regional governments can help improve the productivity of jurisdictions in their areas. Counties encompassing several municipalities or entire metropolitan areas (nearly half the country's metropolitan areas fall within the confines of a single county) might provide or contract services that can be most efficiently produced by a larger government or provided on an areawide basis, such as airport administration, air pollution control, civil defense, transportation, industrial development, sewage disposal, and water supply. Metropolitan authorities, substate regions, or councils of government could similarly promote intergovernmental contracting or other cooperative service arrangements, joint performance measurement systems, or sharing of equipment and expertise.

FEDERAL ACTION TO ENCOURAGE
STATE AND LOCAL GOVERNMENT PRODUCTIVITY

In the United States, 80 percent of the purchases of nondefense goods and services by government, including those heavily financed by the federal government, are administered by states and localities. State and local governments are instruments for carrying out federal policy, spending federal funds, and meeting what are clearly national needs manifested at the local level. These roles are sufficiently important to command federal attention to state and local government productivity.

The federal government has a history of action to improve the performance standards of state and local governments. For example:

> Financing for state employment services in the 1930s was accompanied by a requirement that state administrations install civil service systems, an action hotly opposed at the time by many state officials and politicians.

Planning requirements under the Hospital Survey and Construction Act of 1946 (also known as the Hill-Burton Act) required states to establish state-wide plans for hospital construction based on surveys of needs.

The Housing Act of 1954 required submission of comprehensive "workable programs" as a condition for urban renewal and redevelopment grants. To help states and localities meet these and other planning requirements, the federal government also supplied financial assistance for planning, thereby making possible the great expansion of state and local planning during the 1950s and 1960s.

Although these and related federal actions may have represented institutional improvements at the time, each developed the characteristic difficulties of inflexibility, excessive red tape, and failure to keep up with changing conditions. With the great proliferation of federal grant programs in the 1950s and 1960s, each with its own set of requirements and regulations, federal oversight was increasingly regarded as gratuitous interference in local affairs rather than as a means of ensuring efficient use of federal funds. The most vociferous objections did not concern the establishment of administrative standards so much as the requirements for participation by the poor through community action agencies.

In reaction to the complexity and controversy of the grant programs, the federal government in the 1970s turned to revenue sharing on the assumption that the states and localities were better equipped to ascertain and meet domestic needs for public services.

The resulting spectrum of assistance programs not only fails to use federal influence to raise state and local government productivity but in some ways also impedes improvement. At one end of the spectrum are many categorical grant programs with overly detailed requirements. At the other end is general revenue sharing with few real standards of any kind. In between are the functionally oriented consolidated or block grant programs, covering law enforcement, manpower development, community development, and urban transportation, which are little concerned with overall management improvement. The objective, which is still far from being realized, is a balanced federalism with more flexible federal controls and greater latitude for state and local discretion and innovation. In shifting from one extreme of detailed categorical grants to the other extreme of general revenue sharing with few or no standards, the federal government has skipped over the middle ground of establishing general and flexible standards that encourage productivity.

Restructuring Federal Assistance. We recognize that federal assistance to states and localities serves a variety of purposes and cannot be directed solely to the interest of productivity improvement. However, the power to grant or withhold funds is the most potent source of pressure that can be brought to bear on state and local officials to improve productivity. **We recommend that federal grants, including revenue sharing, block grants, and categorical programs, be redesigned to encourage improvements in the structure and internal management of state and local governments that will enhance productivity.** * Standards for improvement should aim to increase the capacity of states and localities to determine needs and choose courses of action effectively and efficiently; they should not impose the federal will on the states and localities in these matters. There are several options for implementing this recommendation, each of which should be tested and considered in relation to other purposes of federal assistance programs. These options are not necessarily mutually exclusive.

One option is to require that recipients of revenue sharing and block grants meet specified administrative criteria such as comprehensiveness of geographic coverage and powers in given functional areas, effectiveness of general organization, formal representation or access by parties with legitimate interests, adequacy of administrative systems, and the regular compilation of performance data.** Urban transportation grants, for example, might go only to agencies that have metropolitan-wide operations, responsibility for all modes of transportation, formal relationships with general land-use planning bodies in the area, representation of local governments and of state and federal transportation interests, acceptable budgeting and accounting procedures, and regular compilation of data on user need and satisfaction with transportation services. A similar approach was incorporated in a bill sponsored by Congressman Henry S. Reuss and Senator Hubert H. Humphrey in the late 1960s. Aimed at improving the organization and financial operations of state and local government, it would have provided block grants to states having an approved "modern governments program" specifying the state's plan to invigorate and modernize its own government as well as the local governments within the state. In part, it called for reducing the number of overlapping districts, correcting economic disparities among local jurisdictions, and establishing standard machinery of modern organization.

A second option is to require that a specific percentage of federal grants be expended for the development and implementation of techniques to measure, analyze, and improve operations.

*See memorandum by OSCAR A. LUNDIN, page 81.
**See memorandum by CHARLES P. BOWEN, JR., page 82.

A third option is to establish bonus payments for those states and localities that meet specified administrative requirements or develop and implement their own programs for measuring, analyzing, and improving operations.

Finally, for categorical programs in particular, the federal government could place greater emphasis on achieving program objectives and less stress on guidelines and requirements for implementing programs. This would permit flexibility for innovation and adaptation to local conditions while assuring the pursuit of specific federal objectives, which is the purpose of categorical grants.

Administrative standards can encourage better management, but they are of limited efficacy in correcting the deeper problems of administrative arteriosclerosis, indifference, inertia, and lack of incentive for efficient performance. To address these problems, federal assistance programs directed specifically at internal management and productivity improvement are required.

Technical assistance to state and local governments has focused largely on specific functional programs; little or no aid has been provided for general management improvement. A federal interagency committee recently identified eighty major technical assistance programs that in 1974 cost $512 million.[2] Of the total $512 million (1.1 percent of federal grants to states and localities in 1974), about $79 million (only 15 percent of the technical assistance and 0.2 percent of all federal grants) went for general management purposes; most of this was for physical planning and development through the planning grants of the Department of Housing and Urban Development. HUD planning grants and activities under the Intergovernmental Personnel Act have been virtually the only federal programs to address the general management needs of state and local governments, although some agencies recently have initiated so-called capacity-building programs to improve state and local management capability.

One result of the functional orientation of federal technical assistance has been to concentrate the process of designing, managing, and evaluating programs in the functional bureaucracies (health, education, housing, law enforcement, and so forth), each of which forms a loosely integrated verti-

---

2/Study Committee on Policy Management Assistance, *Strengthening Public Management in the Intergovernmental System: A Report Prepared for Office of Management and Budget* (Washington, D.C.: U.S. Government Printing Office, 1975).

cal structure extending from federal to state to local levels. Over the years, this form of functional federalism has had the dual effect of superseding the responsibility of local policy makers in formulating programs to meet community needs and fragmenting local administration along functional lines to the detriment of coordinated service delivery.

We recommend that federal financial and technical assistance to state and local governments for improving internal management be expanded. An important source of expertise in this area is the federal government's program to improve its own productivity.

The federal assistance program has suffered from a general lack of leadership, the absence of coordination among agencies providing assistance, and the failure to involve state and local officials themselves in the design of programs. The Advisory Commission on Intergovernmental Relations has made numerous recommendations for strengthening the federal system in general and the grant program in particular, but ACIR lacks the authority for establishing or implementing policy. **We recommend that the President designate a federal agency to develop policy and coordinate implementation of federal assistance to states and localities with the participation of state and local officials. This agency should have direct access to the chief executive.*** The agency should both address the productivity implications of federal assistance and be responsible for strengthening management in the intergovernmental system.**

For example, a series of steps could be taken to improve the administration of general grant programs, including reducing the complexity of applications, cutting the time that elapses between filing of applications and awarding of grants, permitting consolidated application for several grants in related areas, and improving the effectiveness of the Federal Regional Councils in grant administration. A recent report noted related deficiencies in federal grant procedures.[3] Some progress has been made in correcting them, but additional improvement is still possible.

Improving Public-Sector Manpower Policy. There are numerous impediments to the effective use of personnel in state and local government, some of which could be alleviated by federal action. Rigidities in

---

3/Comptroller General of the United States, *Fundamental Changes Are Needed in Federal Assistance to State and Local Governments: Report to the Congress* (Washington, D.C.: U.S. General Accounting Office, 1975).

*See memorandum by R. STEWART RAUCH, JR., page 82.
**See memorandum by OSCAR A. LUNDIN, page 82.

civil service systems inhibit the productive use of manpower within governments and, especially as a result of the nonportability of pensions, impede the distribution of professional skills to assignments and jurisdictions where they are most needed. For example, although federal policy, as reflected in revenue sharing, is attempting to shift financial resources and greater responsibility to the state and local levels, there is no commensurate effort to redistribute the substantial talent in the federal government to state and local governments where it is most needed. Recruitment and training are undertaken on a jurisdiction-by-jurisdiction basis without the benefit of national mechanisms to facilitate the identification and development of management talent. Relatively little has been done to encourage personnel interchanges between the public and private sectors that could bring business experience to government, and vice versa (as, for example, in the Executive Interchange Program for the federal government).

We recommend that the Intergovernmental Personnel Act (IPA) programs of interchange among federal, state, and local governments be expanded and, in addition, that interchanges between the private and public sectors be promoted. We further recommend that the U.S. Civil Service Commission's Bureau of Intergovernmental Personnel Programs or the National Commission for Manpower Policy undertake a major review of public-sector manpower policy in order to determine ways to make state and local civil service and personnel systems more conducive to productivity improvement and to examine possibilities for nationwide mechanisms of recruitment, interchange, and pension portability for state and local personnel.

We also urge that federal agencies make a practice of assigning officials who are responsible for grant programs to work in states and localities for limited periods as a means of both providing technical assistance and expanding their understanding of state and local conditions and operating problems. In such assignments and in IPA interchange programs, measures should be taken to discourage the practice of assigning less effective personnel to state and local positions.

More Effective Innovation, Research, and Development. Many state and local governments are disinclined to experiment with new techniques and develop new technologies. The Federal Council for Science and Technology noted in 1972 that use of science and technology by state and local governments was roughly equivalent to that of the federal government in 1940, that is, largely dependent on external resources for research and development.

The federal government can play an important role in providing both funds and stimulus for research and innovation. However, federal efforts to date have suffered from poor design, methods, and evaluation because of a lack of planning and overdependence on random innovation. Such federal programs as Community Action, Model Cities, and Title III of the Elementary and Secondary Education Act of 1965 relied heavily on local experimentation without systematic approaches or evaluation that would have increased their usefulness. From their point of view, state and local officials complain that some federal research affecting their interests does not involve them in either design or implementation.

SYSTEMATIC EXPERIMENTATION

In Kansas City, an experiment initiated by local police personnel and sponsored by the Police Foundation investigated the effectiveness of conventional random police patrol on the crime rate and citizens' sense of security in three districts of the city. In one district, police patrols were quadrupled; in a second, patrols were held at customary levels; in a third, patrols were eliminated, and police responded only to specific calls for service. One year's experience indicated no difference in either the crime rate or the citizens' perceptions of their own safety, suggesting that there may be more effective ways to use police officers in large cities than random patrol.

Some attempts have been made to draw upon federal research and development in space and defense for application to the cities, but in general, such efforts have been piecemeal and have overemphasized the adaptation of hardware. A more far-reaching approach is required to reorient the massive federal investment in research and development to serve the needs of state and local governments more effectively.

Federal research has also been deficient in the dissemination of results. This stems partly from failure to involve potential users (state and local officials) in important research efforts, but it also reflects distorted budget priorities. This suggests not simply publishing more reports but also determining more imaginative ways both to reach potential users and to increase their desire for new techniques and knowledge.

One example of lost opportunity has been research and demonstration in mass transportation. The congressional Office of Technology Assessment, noting that transit technology has made little advance in the last fifty years, has criticized the federal program for failure to identify transit needs precisely and to evolve systems for meeting needs; for overemphasis on esoteric new systems that do not address themselves to existing transit problems; and for overemphasis on transit hardware generally, as opposed to experimentation with service levels, fare structures, and other matters concerning the convenience and availability of mass transit. The emphasis on transit hardware has been criticized as being solutions in search of problems.

We recommend that federally sponsored research and development be restructured to devote a larger share of resources to problems facing state and local governments in a way that would involve state and local officials in identifying priorities and approaches, emphasizing systematic experimentation, and improving the dissemination of results.

Leadership for Improvement. In the end, a more effective federal role in improving government productivity at the state and local levels requires national institutional commitment and leadership. Despite many obstacles, including congressional apathy, the National Commission on Productivity and Work Quality made an effective start by publicizing the importance of improving public-sector productivity and initiating projects to define and stimulate local government productivity. **We recommend that the President and Congress demonstrate their concern for improving state and local government productivity through support of an effective federal effort to provide leadership, coordination among federal agencies, and involvement and stimulation of state and local governments. We applaud the conversion of the National Commission on Productivity and Work Quality into the permanent National Center for Productivity and Quality of Working Life. However, to be effective, the new center requires funding substantially beyond its current annual appropriation of $2 million.*** This center should continue to emphasize the improvement of public-sector productivity. The federal government's experience in improving its own productivity should be adopted by the new center for application to state and local governments.

*See memorandum by R. HEATH LARRY, page 83.

Memoranda of Comment, Reservation, or Dissent

Page 11, by FRANKLIN A. LINDSAY

The report gives inadequate weight to the limitations on productivity improvement often imposed by state legislatures. These limitations arise when legislators fail to appreciate the counterproductive effects of overly restrictive legislation and when special interests use the legislative route to frustrate the efforts of public executives to reform or cut back marginal activities or to reduce inefficiencies and duplication.

Page 14, by CHARLES P. BOWEN, JR.

Except for bond issues, few citizens have an opportunity to know the relationships or make or express a choice between cost, as represented by taxes, and service. This applies whether the service is for the entire community or for special groups of citizens.

Apparently the overriding objective of many of our political representatives and governmental servants is to keep it this way and to confuse, not clarify, those relationships. Hence, the growing popularity of the so-called transfer payments, an anesthetic form of taxation.

We should advocate much more detailed analysis and publication of programs, unit costs of sources, and recipients of tax revenue and of their comparison with other communities. Citizens so informed might then have some reasonable basis for assessing and expressing how real some of their needs are. They have no such basis now.

Page 16, by MARK SHEPHERD, JR.

This report has correctly identified local goal setting as a vital element in overall productivity improvement. But local goal setting must derive from a community consensus and compromise of many special interests. One important local attempt to develop community goals was the Goals for Dallas program instituted in Dallas, Texas, under Mayor Erik Jonsson in 1965. The supporting organization continues to exist today. The local city manager still finds the path eased for introduction of programs that correspond to Goals for Dallas targets because a local basis of popular support for them has already been developed. Further, this program led to the widespread use of goal-setting techniques in the city government and institutionalized consultation with citizens on city goals.

Pages 22 and 67, by OSCAR A. LUNDIN

Implicit in the entire section regarding federal responsibility and actions appears to be the assumption that there is a greater percentage of federal employees with management expertise than there is at the state and local level. This assumption results in the recommendation that the federal government provide expert technical assistance to improve internal management in state and local government.

To me, that assumption is not valid. I am not aware any data exist to show that the federal government has a greater percentage of employees competent in the field of management. Because of the greater number of employees at the state and local level, it is very likely there is a greater number of such employees having competency in management than at the federal level.

To the extent that existing federal expertise in improving productivity can be passed along to state and local governments, it should be done, provided it is done in a manner that avoids the federal government dictating to the others. Moreover, it should be emphasized the federal government probably would be able to learn from the expertise available in the states.

Pages 22 and 67, by OSCAR A. LUNDIN

I strongly support the concept of improving productivity at the state and local government levels and commend the growing number of political entities that have already taken steps in this direction. This is an important area in which I believe too little attention has been focused. Therefore, I am in agreement with the recommendations which encourage those governments to take the initiative in improving their productivity.

However, I am concerned with those recommendations and statements regarding federal responsibility and actions to improve state and local government productivity. In my view, there already has been too much federal intrusion into lower levels of government. Some of the recommendations contained in the report would, I believe, cause further intrusion.

Pages 23 and 69, by FRAZAR B. WILDE

The implications of this recommendation extend far beyond productivity into basic social change. While much of this change is necessary and desirable, the open-endedness of this recommendation troubles me.

Pages 23 and 70, by FRAZAR B. WILDE

I concur with this recommendation as it relates to preserving employee benefits. Beyond this, however, mobility of employment without loss of rank or seniority is, in my judgment, counterproductive.

Pages 23 and 70, by FRAZAR B. WILDE

I think this recommendation should be modified to provide that any such set of minimum standards be designed in a manner to differentiate appropriately among the various sizes of local governments. In small communities, I think that government is still close to the citizenry and that productivity is good. To impose a heavy set of bureaucratic standards on small communities, as states have a tendency to do, is counterproductive.

Pages 24 and 73, by OSCAR A. LUNDIN

This paragraph of the report indicates that the federal government should "encourage" the state and local governments to improve productivity. This can be done because "the power to grant or withhold funds is the most potent source of pressure that can be brought to bear on state and local officials to improve productivity." This is contradicted by the sentence which states that standards for improving productivity "should not impose the federal will on the states and localities in these matters." Despite this contradiction, the thrust appears to be forcing state and local governments to do what is dictated by the federal government. I find this unacceptable.

Pages 24 and 73, by CHARLES P. BOWEN, JR., *with which* CHARLES C. TILLING-HAST, JR., *has asked to be associated*

I strongly disagree with using federal revenue sharing as a weapon to force local adoption of federal concepts of good management practices. The entire revenue sharing program is a totally inadequate patchwork substitute for correction of a basic tax policy error. That error has led to too much federal, as opposed to local, taxation. Substantial abdication of local control over levels and methods of taxation and over effective expenditure of tax funds is the natural result.

Revenue sharing is a prime example of the negative impact upon good management practices of transfer payment programs which obscure the relationship between revenue sources and revenue expenditure beneficiaries. It encourages communities to make commitments for more than they have the resources to support.

Rather than seeking to increase federal impact for what are admittedly good ends, we should consider the inherent inefficiencies of this increased centralization of power and the resulting duplication of expensive organization structures. There is nothing in recent history to demonstrate that the federal government is the source of all, or even most, of the good management answers. The closer we can place control of expenditures to the people who pay for them, the more likely we are to reduce them and to get more value for what is spent.

Pages 25 and 75, by OSCAR A. LUNDIN

The report recommends that the President designate a single federal agency with direct access to him to develop policy and coordinate implementation of federal assistance to states with participation of state and local officials. This recommendation in my view would likely create another layer of bureaucracy at the federal level and inhibit rather than promote the federal assistance desired. I suggest some independent group (such as the Advisory Commission on Intergovernmental Relations) should be charged with the responsibility of trying to improve productivity at all levels of government, federal as well as state and local. Funding for such a group might be provided by foundations.

Pages 25 and 75, by R. STEWART RAUCH, JR.

This recommendation or designation of a particular federal agency to develop management policies and administrative standards is a narrow solution for a pervasive problem and is likely to be counterproductive. Every agency of the federal government, including Congress, should understand and respond to the need for program efficiency. "Designation" of one federal agency makes it convenient for others to ignore the issues. Moreover, the major flow of policy initiatives should be from state and local governments to federal agencies, not, as this recommendation too strongly implies, the other way around. Creation of a bureaucratic vested interest in this matter within the federal government may well become obstructive of local experimentation.

Pages 26 and 78, by R. HEATH LARRY

Although the current fiscal year 1976 appropriation for the center remains at the $2 million level ascribed to the former National Commission on Productivity and Work Quality, the legislation creating the National Center for Productivity and Quality of Working Life, P.L. 94-136, authorizes an annual spending ceiling of $5 million for three years. As a member of the former productivity commission and a counselor to the vice-president in his capacity as chairman of the center, I want to note that additional financial resources would permit the center to address more specific sectors of the economy. It intends to work in close cooperation with other agencies to increase the total amount of federal resources available for productivity improvement. The role of the center is, and ought to be, primarily catalytic.

The importance of external pressures to achieve greater performance accountability by public officials cannot be underscored sufficiently. In the exercise of this pressure, private organizations and individuals must keep in mind that the most significant productivity gains for the nation as a whole may require redistribution of traditionally public functions to other sectors of the economy, and in some cases, it may even require the elimination of certain governmental activities, for example, those regulations that protect a few at great economic cost. The process of achieving *efficiency* in the conduct of *appropriate* governmental functions will require change that may impact all of us. Those of us external to government must realize that public-sector productivity improvement is our responsibility as well.

Page 31, by MARK SHEPHERD, JR.

Education represents one-third of state and local government expenditures. This is obviously one area where productivity improvements could have a major impact on state and local budgets but where very little progress has been made; indeed, few educators in the profession appear to be thinking of productivity improvement as a critical goal. In the 1973 Carnegie-Mellon University Benjamin F. Fairless Lectures, Patrick E. Haggerty has discussed this issue of educational productivity in greater detail. See *The Productive Society* (New York: Columbia University Press, 1974).

84

Page 39, by CHARLES P. BOWEN, JR., *with which* CHARLES C. TILLINGHAST, JR., *has asked to be associated*

I don't believe we should accept at face value this glib explanation of the sources of crime. Countries with unemployment and poverty levels far worse than ours neither experience nor tolerate violent criminal practices we are urged to accept as inevitable because of economic inequities.

The real issue is that our culture has long been implicitly encouraged by too many irresponsible sociologists, educators, and politicians to accept permissive and irresponsible personal behavior as normal. These same sources champion the civil rights of criminals without much consideration of the civil rights of their victims. The resulting ineffective police, judicial, and correctional practices make violent crime appear to be attractively risk-free.

Until we get at that root of the problem, improvements in police efficiency are of doubtful significance.

Page 39, by JAMES Q. RIORDAN, *with which* C. WREDE PETERSMEYER *and* CHARLES C. TILLINGHAST, JR., *have asked to be associated*

I do not approve the statement *Improving Productivity in State and Local Government.*

History and logic strongly suggest that productivity of government varies in inverse ratio with its scope and size. The possibility that the government's size and scope should be reduced is virtually ignored in the report. The fact is that government efficiency and effectiveness will never reach their highest possible levels. This is true for all systems and institutions. If private philanthropy reached its highest possible levels, there would be less need for government welfare; if private morality and self-discipline reached their highest levels, there would be less need for police. Nevertheless, all would agree that government should supply welfare and police service based on our experience to date with private philanthropy and morality. The problem is: How big should today's imperfect government be in today's imperfect world? One possible answer may be: *smaller.*

Appendix A   PENNSYLVANIA PROGRAM BUDGETING SYSTEM

THE FOLLOWING EXAMPLE illustrates how one state's program budgeting system focuses decision making on the impacts and outputs of programs and how it requires analysis to support budget requests.

BUDGET FORMAT

Pennsylvania's program budget classifies all state activities within a four-level program structure: state programs, program categories, program subcategories, and elements. The state police function falls within the state program "Protection of Persons and Property," and the agency activities are classified into five program categories, one of which is "Traffic Safety and Supervision." This category is, in turn, broken down into three subcategories, one of which is "Traffic Supervision." The program measures include both impact data (effect of the activities upon fatalities and injuries), which provide a basis for effectiveness analysis, and output data (such as number of arrests).

APPROPRIATIONS HEARING

The following excerpt from one of the Pennsylvania House Appropriations Committee hearings with the state police dealing with the "Traffic Supervision" subcategory illustrates the growing interest of state legislators in more systematically assessing program effectiveness.

Excerpt from The Pennsylvania House Appropriations Committee Hearings, April 2, 1975

Chairman Wojdak: I had asked several questions about the means of collecting data, hard data, to establish and determine the effectiveness of certain programs. One was . . . traffic supervision. . . . I would like you to furnish me as soon as possible with how you are determining the effectiveness of these programs and if you have no means at present of determining the effectiveness, how you plan to determine the effectiveness of it. . . .

Major Buchinsky: Yes. I did want to offer something, Mr. Chairman, if I may. I don't know who put some of these statements in and that is concerning the low number of accidents and the fact that patrols do not have a major impact on accident rate. I would like to find where the reference is. In other words, what documentation there is to support that general statement for this particular reason. . . .

Chairman Wojdak: Major, everything you say may very well be true. My question was to determine on the basis of what some recent studies have shown and we will furnish those to you if you want them.

Major Buchinsky: I would appreciate that.

Chairman Wojdak: Okay. That patrolling really was not a significant factor in reducing the occurrence of accidents. Now, you may disagree with that. We will furnish you with those studies.

My questions to you before were what considerations you were using in determining how many numbers of officers you would use in traffic control . . . in light of these studies.

Major Buchinsky: May I cite one particular instance where the presence of other patrols would have gone ahead and prevented a fatality?

Chairman Wojdak: There is no doubt in my mind that in individual cases, and I am not certain how many cases that would be or what percentage it would be, I am certain there are instances where patrol does prevent accidents.

Major Buchinsky: And this is one that we could document very definitely, sir. . . .

Chairman Wojdak: I think everyone's ultimate goal is running things most efficiently and if, in fact, studies show that . . . traffic patrols don't have a major impact on accidents, all I am really trying to determine is what alternative plans, or how that affects your thinking in allocating officers because ultimately, if you disagree with the plan, your requests will be for additional officers.

All I am trying to determine is what your thinking is and it is the same thing with the determination of the effectiveness of the municipal police training program and with the crime prevention program.

PROGRAM ANALYSIS ABSTRACT

Results of an analysis conducted by the Program Planning and Evaluation unit in the Governor's Budget Office are being used to revise their 1976-1977 budget request. The study examined the relation between traffic accidents and enforcement by state police. This state activity spends approximately $67 million per year attempting to minimize accidents.

The data were collected at eighteen locations across the state. The researchers employed a random sampling technique in gathering the data. The major analytic techniques were correlation analysis and stepwise multiple regression analysis.

Based on the results of the correlation analysis and the experience of other studies in the field, the following were chosen as the independent variables: traffic volume, total arrests, patrol hours, radar hours, season, highway type, and zone number. The major dependent variable was total traffic accidents. Other dependent variables investigated were accidents specific with respect to severity and highway type. The results are summarized below:

1. The analysis definitely indicates a relation between the level of enforcement and total traffic accidents. It can be stated that if the state police increase in-view patrol hours, the effect will be a depressing effect on total accidents.

   This statement does not imply that an increase in patrol hours will result in an absolute decline in traffic accidents. It does state that an increase in patrol hours will result in fewer accidents than would have occurred otherwise. This qualification is made necessary by the powerful impact of traffic volume on the accident rate.

2. Total arrests are also a significant depressant of total accidents. However, as the analysis becomes specific to type of accident and highway type, the significance dissolves. The signs, though, are consistent, indicating that the state police are having the desired effect.

3. Radar hours are generally an insignificant explainer of total accidents and accidents specific to severity and highway type. However, the signs of the coefficients do indicate that the very weak relationship is in the desired direction; that is, radar hours suppress accidents. As is pointed out above, the weakness of the radar hours relationship is partially accounted for by the limits of the data set.

Problem	*Measure*	*Type of Change*
Backlog of reports and documents to be typed	Lines typed per week, cost savings	Technological improvement
Excessive time spent investigating building department complaints not in violation of law	Percentage of valid violation cases inspected, number of inspections per case	Rescheduling of activities
Delay in patient care at a county medical center emergency room	Time required for processing patients	Redeployment of staff
Inability to investigate and recertify monthly social services case load	Number of cases com- pleted, number of cases completed per examiner per month	Reassignment of tasks
High percentage of trucks to be repaired	Number of vehicles repaired, time vehicles are out of operation	Rescheduling of activities and inventory control

[1]Method of evaluation developed and used in Nassau and Westchester Counties, New York.

▪scription of Change	Result
▪ord-processing center to allow ▪r machine dictation and faster ▪ing	Reorganization of typing pool from forty-one to seventeen typists
▪ssignment of inspectors to the ▪fice one day per week to screen ▪ilding department cases	Reduction in the number of no-violation cases inspected and increases in the number of cases closed
▪iage nurse to screen cases, ▪velopment of walk-in clinic during ▪eak hours to handle nonemergency ▪ases, establishment of new shifts ▪r nurses to match staffing with ▪atient demand	Decrease in the average waiting and treatment time for patients
▪onsolidation of units, specialization ▪f duties to free examiner's time ▪r fieldwork, equalization of workload, ▪tandardization of tasks, increased ▪upervisory support	21.3 percent increase in the number of cases completed per examiner per month
▪reventive-maintenance program that ▪ncludes: inventory control, scheduling ▪f vehicles for repair and inspection, ▪ducation program for personnel on ▪roper use of trucks, night shift ▪reated (responsible for preventive ▪naintenance of trucks)	13 percent decrease in time vehicles are out of service

Appendix C MANAGEMENT INFORMATION SYSTEM DEVELOPMENT AND APPLICATION

THE DEVELOPMENT of a management information system (MIS) in Sunnyvale, California, can be traced through four distinct stages.

Stage One: Reporting. During the initial period, Sunnyvale used essentially the same management information and reporting system that the majority of municipalities used up until the late 1960s: a line-item budget, with expenditures being the only quantifiable measure of performance and accounting records the only reporting mechanism. This system was not particularly useful in either planning or controlling municipal operations. It had no capability for performance assessment, and overall management and planning with this type of system was a day-to-day affair.

Stage Two: Measuring. In this stage, the information system moved to a line-item budget summarized by programs. Program managers began to define the outputs of the major functions. Control measures were aggregated to unit-cost indicators. The system operated in this manner while the on-line management information modules were being developed by the management staff and the software contractor. Top management could use unit-cost indicators as control mechanisms for programs within each of the functions. The elected officials were now able to review a budget that more accurately reflected the effect of expenditures on municipal functions. During the latter part of this period, the council decided that the parallel line-item budget was unnecessary and dropped it during the review process.

Stage Three: Planning. The third stage initially included bringing on line the real-time management information system of the accounting, personnel, payroll, and utility accounting modules; implementing a long-range capital budgeting system; and beginning PPBS. Later, the six additional modules for purchasing, inventory, equipment control, fixed-asset accounting, public safety, and library were brought on line.

Stage Four: Predicting and Controlling. Now in the development process, this stage is an MIS with a metropolitan data base. Information would be used to predict and control the impact of the municipal policy decisions on individual citizens and other government units within the area. To reach this stage, new intergovernmental coalitions must be formed to develop the data base required for such a system. When this system is fully developed, governments will be able to respond to the needs and demands of their citizens with a coordinated approach based on information that is both current and reliable and that adequately represents the impact of an action on the entire metropolitan area.

Source: Joint Financial Management Improvement Program, *Annual Report to the President and the Congress: Productivity Programs in the Federal Government FY 1974,* vol. 2, *Case Studies* (Washington, D.C., June 1975).

Objectives of the Committee for Economic Development

For three decades, the Committee for Economic Development has had a respected influence on business and public policy. Composed of two hundred leading business executives and educators, CED is devoted to these two objectives:

To develop, through objective research and informed discussion, findings and recommendations for private and public policy which will contribute to preserving and strengthening our free society, achieving steady economic growth at high employment and reasonably stable prices, increasing productivity and living standards, providing greater and more equal opportunity for every citizen, and improving the quality of life for all.

To bring about increasing understanding by present and future leaders in business, government, and education and among concerned citizens of the importance of these objectives and the ways in which they can be achieved.

CED's work is supported strictly by private voluntary contributions from business and industry, foundations, and individuals. It is independent, nonprofit, nonpartisan, and nonpolitical.

The two hundred trustees, who generally are presidents or board chairmen of corporations and presidents of universities, are chosen for their individual capacities rather than as representatives of any particular interests. By working with scholars, they unite business judgment and experience with scholarship in analyzing the issues and developing recommendations to resolve the economic problems that constantly arise in a dynamic and democratic society.

Through this business-academic partnership, CED endeavors to develop policy statements and other research materials that commend themselves as guides to public and business policy; for use as texts in college economics and political science courses and in management training courses; for consideration and discussion by newspaper and magazine editors, columnists, and commentators; and for distribution abroad to promote better understanding of the American economic system.

CED believes that by enabling businessmen to demonstrate constructively their concern for the general welfare, it is helping business to earn and maintain the national and community respect essential to the successful functioning of the free enterprise capitalist system.

Social Responsibilities of Business Corporations (*June 1971*)

Education for the Urban Disadvantaged:
  From Preschool to Employment (*March 1971*)

Further Weapons Against Inflation (*November 1970*)

Making Congress More Effective (*September 1970*)

*Development Assistance to Southeast Asia (*July 1970*)

Training and Jobs for the Urban Poor (*July 1970*)

Improving the Public Welfare System (*April 1970*)

Reshaping Government in Metropolitan Areas (*February 1970*)

Economic Growth in the United States (*October 1969*)

Assisting Development in Low-Income Countries (*September 1969*)

*Nontariff Distortions of Trade (*September 1969*)

Fiscal and Monetary Policies for Steady Economic Growth (*January 1969*)

Financing a Better Election System (*December 1968*)

Innovation in Education: New Directions for the American School (*July 1968*)

Modernizing State Government (*July 1967*)

*Trade Policy Toward Low-Income Countries (*June 1967*)

How Low Income Countries Can Advance Their Own Growth (*September 1966*)

Modernizing Local Government (*July 1966*)

A Better Balance in Federal Taxes on Business (*April 1966*)

Budgeting for National Objectives (*January 1966*)

Presidential Succession and Inability (*January 1965*)

Educating Tomorrow's Managers (*October 1964*)

Improving Executive Management in the Federal Government (*July 1964*)

Trade Negotiations for a Better Free World Economy (*May 1964*)

Union Powers and Union Functions: Toward a Better Balance (*March 1964*)

Japan in the Free World Economy (*April 1963*)

Economic Literacy for Americans (*March 1962*)

Statements issued in association with CED counterpart organizations in foreign countries.

DATE DUE